MW01017392

Equicapita's
LITTLE BOOK OF
WHAT
Next?

The entrepreneur's guide to preparing,
structuring and negotiating the
successful sale of your business

Dedications

Greg would like to dedicate this book to Janet, Reid, Spencer and his parents: kindness, perseverance and self-belief will take you a long way. Thank you to my wonderfully weird family for always being in my corner! Most importantly, never listen to 'Stan'...

Michael would like to dedicate this book to Stacie, Lexi, Ruby and Sam – for their love, support, patience and inspiration. Thanks to Mom and Dad for their support. Thanks also to all the business owners with whom we deal – we are always impressed with what you have accomplished.

Stephen would like to dedicate this book to Willem, Libby and Connor – the next generation.

Thomas would like to dedicate this book to his colleagues (past and present) for the opportunity to be a part of this. Thank-you for your support, enthusiasm and wisdom.

Copyright Equicapita 2014

First Published in September 2014

ISBN-13: 9781502338211

Printed in Canada

All rights reserved

Second Edition

Contents

Prologue

I t has been said that demographics are destiny. By now, no business owner should be surprised that the West (Western Hemisphere that is) is facing a wave of retirements as the Baby Boom generation moves to the end of their working careers.[1]

Just how large is the trend? In 2000, the ratio of Americans between 15 and 59 years old to those over 60 was four to one, according to a United Nations report. In 2050, the ratio will be only two to one. In Canada the story is much the same. By approximately 2015 Canada will have more people leaving the labor force than joining. Retirees are expected to exceed 40% of the Canadian working age population by the mid-2010s. This is the largest ratio of retirees to working age population and quickly approaching one retiree for every two working age person.

The good news is that the emerging markets in aggregate will not face the West's demographic challenge for several decades and so at the margin will remain a strong source of incremental demand for certain sectors of the economy (particularly the commodity sector). The emerging markets currently have a dependency ratio (the ratio of dependents to working-age citizens) roughly equal to the developed markets. However, this overlooks the composition of the dependents:

According to the United Nations, the current dependency ratio is about even at 62% for both developing and developed nations. An important difference between developing and developed countries is the type of dependents: The majority of non-workers in developed countries are past the working age; the majority of non-workers in developing countries are not yet old enough to enter the workforce. Based on the United Nations' projection of demographic trends to

2050, emerging countries are poised to gain a substantial advantage over developed ones.[2]

This demographic advantage is expected to emerge quite soon - by 2016, the dependency ratio in developed markets will be higher than that of emerging markets and growing faster.

Returning to western demographics, what is the single largest baby boomer retirement issue or concern? Is it pension solvency, retirement savings levels, healthcare funding? All very important, however one issue that is rarely discussed in the media is: Where will the capital come from to acquire the large cohort of private, baby-boomer businesses coming onto the market? What effect is this going to have on baby boomer entrepreneurs who will be considering the sale of their businesses as one option on a path to retirement? Will they find that without the ability to sell their businesses for reasonable valuations they may struggle to fund their retirements?

A recent CIBC report estimated that "$1.9 trillion in business assets are poised to change hands in five years - the biggest transfer of Canadian business control on record." and "by 2022, this number will mushroom to at least $3.7 trillion as 550,000 owners exit their businesses..."[3] So how will this large cohort of entrepreneurs exit and at what price?

The question will come down in part to the amount of acquisition capital flowing into the private small business space. Given that this estimated $2 trillion of Canadian small businesses is twice as large as the assets of the top 1,000 Canadian pension plans and approximately the same size as Canadian annual GDP this is a question without an obvious answer. [4,5] This mismatch between deal supply and capital creates interesting opportunities and challenges for both buyers and sellers alike in the market at the sub-$20 million acquisition size.

Another issue to note is that the process of selling a private business can take up to 3 years from the date that the decision is made to pursue a sale to the final closing. The time to start planning is now. Especially as a baby-boomer entrepreneur you are facing a potential competitive environment in which to sell your business.

The purpose of the this book is to provide guidance on best practices and background into what acquirers will look for in your business and from that how they will ultimately arrive at a valuation. We have included examples to help reinforce key messages. As well, you will notice some duplication of certain discussion points; again, this was intentional so as to reinforce those key messages. We have also sprinkled a liberal dose of quotes that we hope you find interesting and perhaps even inspirational.

Forearmed with the information in this book you are more likely to generate a sales price that most accurately reflects the intrinsic value of your business and save valuable time and energy in the process.

Action is the foundational key to all success.

– Pablo Picasso

There is only one boss. The customer. And he can fire everybody in the company from the chairman on down, simply by spending his money somewhere else.

– *Sam Walton*

CHAPTER 1

Why Most Businesses Never Sell

A wise man will make
more opportunities
than he finds.

– *Francis Bacon*

necdotally, up to 20% of all businesses are "for sale" at any given time and of those businesses for sale, only 25% ever sell. While this data may not be strictly empirical, it is reflective of our collective experience in the market.

What this means is that of the nearly 70% of business owners expecting to sell their businesses over the next 10 years in Canada, only 25% of those will actually sell. This of course assumes that the success rate does not in fact decrease below 25% as more businesses come on the market.

Why is the success rate so low? While there are many reasons businesses do not ultimately sell, at the top of the list are the following:

1. A lack of understanding of how businesses are valued, resulting in unrealistic pricing expectations,

2. A lack of understanding of the sales process, including not understanding the purchaser's objectives and requirements,

3. Not having a management succession plan, and

4. Not running the company as a business but rather as a 'job' for the owner.

Understanding how businesses are valued

Owners who do not have an accurate idea of what their business is really worth often feel insulted when they receive an offer and it is lower than what they think it should be. What a business is worth from the eyes of a business owner, particularly one that started the business from scratch, often differs substantially from what a buyer believes it is "worth" and is ultimately willing to pay. As a result, what commonly results is an inability to get a deal done as the gap in pricing expectations is too wide.

Understanding the sale process

Another common mistake is that owners go about the sales process in entirely the wrong way - and by the wrong way, we mean that businesses are often inappropriately positioned with prospective purchasers, management is not kept in mind as to the future plans for the business and the business does not get properly prepared for the sale process. When we use the phrase inappropriately positioned we mean that too many businesses are marketed in such a generic manner that no real information is provided on why the business is a great acquisition opportunity. The best way to position a business for sale is similar to any sales process, *"sell the sizzle"*, meaning market the benefits or key features that exist in the business.

For example, as opposed to showing the growth profile of the business as a simple but uninspiring table of dry financial information, instead show the profile of the top 20 customers over the last 3 years to illustrate how the amounts of business with these customers has increased and how the percentage of overall sales attributable to these customers has decreased demonstrating increased customer diversity and increased customer penetration at the same time.

Another example is a detailed analysis of the components of cost of goods sold over the past three years to illustrate how improvements in the purchasing department, combined with efficiencies realized in operations have led to reduced cost of sales and increased gross margins. This not only shows higher profits but also shows concrete examples of a well run, constantly improving business.

These are the type of data points investors look for when making investment decisions. To present them in a compelling fashion in marketing documents makes the process easier for the investing professionals and also helps separate the wheat from the chaff.

Management succession planning

It is estimated that half of Canadian small-business owners plan to retire and transfer control of their business by 2019[6] while typically only 10% of all independent business owners have a formal plan to sell or transfer their business. Having a succession plan will help ensure a business transition goes as smoothly as possible. A well-designed succession plan will help:

- Ensure the future financial stability and value of the business.

- Reduce the potential tax liabilities of transferring the ownership.

- Set a timetable for transfer of ownership to the successor, whether a family member, employee or an outside purchaser.

- Contribute to the growth of the business in terms of market share, profitability and size.

- Provide stability for employees.

Running the company as a business

What does this mean? Often what appears to be a business is really just a job for the owner – i.e. without the owner present and working constantly the "business" cannot continue. A company operating this way is not an appealing acquisition for a financial investor. There are a number of things that can be done to avoid this including documenting systems and processes and training strong managers who can step into the role of the founder.

Pay attention to those employees who respectfully ask why. They are demonstrating an interest in their jobs and exhibiting a curiosity that could eventually translate into leadership ability.

— *Harvey Mackay*

CHAPTER 2

Your Options

If you decide to sell your business and it is inadequately marketed, inappropriately represented or improperly valued, the business will likely not sell.

–Equicapita

While this book is clearly focused on selling your business, it is important to understand that selling your business is not your only option. While we believe in most cases the sale of your business may be the best course of action, in many cases other options may be viable and preferable. At a high level your options as the owner of a business are:

1. Sell

2. Continue to run with significant involvement – never retire

3 Have someone run it in your place

4. Pursue a growth strategy

5. Wind-down and liquidate

The purpose of the following chapters is to work through the process of the "sell" option as we believe this is ultimately the best approach to allow a founder/entrepreneur to transition to retirement. We also provide a brief overview of the pursuit of a growth strategy.

Judge a man by his questions rather than his answers.

– Voltaire

Economic progress is the work of the savers, who accumulate capital, and of the entrepreneurs, who turn capital to new uses. The other members of society, of course, enjoy the advantages of progress, but they not only do not contribute anything to it; they even place obstacles in its way.

– *Ludvig von Mises*

CHAPTER 3

Selling Your Business – Where to Start?

Business is not just doing deals; business is having great products, doing great engineering, and providing tremendous service to customers. Finally, business is a cobweb of human relationships.

– Ross Perot

ince you will only sell your business once, it goes without saying you will want to ensure that the transaction goes smoothly and that you achieve the highest price possible. The factors outlined in this chapter will provide insight into the best ways to ensure your business sells and you receive maximum value.

Find an advisor

Let us be explicit, if you decide to sell your business and it is inadequately marketed, inappropriately represented or improperly valued, the likelihood of it selling is low. Anecdotally you can see this effect in the market. As previously noted, as many as 20% (one in five) private businesses are for sale at any one time and of those for sale, only 25% of those are ever sold and the business owner fully divested. The others are either shut down and the assets liquidated or the business owner continues to be significantly involved in the day-to-day operations well beyond his or her retirement age.

If you have a likely purchaser or partner lined up where you expect to complete a deal, it is important to have advisors (legal, accounting and tax) that you can rely on to help guide you through the transaction process. This includes ensuring your advisors have expertise in actual private company transactions and being aware of your individual financial requirements, tax implications and legal nuances of a private company deal.

There exists an extensive network of mergers and acquisitions advisors who specialize in working with owners to position a business for sale, produce valuations, manage the sale process and assist in the negotiations with the potential purchaser. Do not hesitate to contact a few and have them pitch you on their services. Your relationship with your advisor, if you choose to go this route, will be key to the outcome. Make sure to get someone experienced and with whom you have a positive, productive working relationship.

How the business is positioned and marketed can be as important to the ultimate sale outcome as the quality of the business itself. Ensure the firm you choose to represent you for your sale transaction has a proven system and a successful track record – do your due diligence on potential advisors, ask for examples, or references, of other successful transactions and/or similar companies they have successfully represented.

The reason we are stressing the management of the sale process is that without this, the process can go on for a protracted period of time. You do not want your business to be perpetually on the market. If you work with a firm with a proven system for getting results your ultimate success is greatly improved.

A major issue faced by successors or third party purchasers of the business is the financing of the acquisition. Often financing conditions are required by the purchaser in the form of external bank financing – many deals fall apart when the purchaser cannot source debt financing in time to close or is turned down entirely. When selling your business, ensure that you are represented by sophisticated advisors who are familiar with structuring acquisition financing so that they can provide guidance to both you and the purchaser in ensuring the deal will be successfully completed. Also deal with an advisor that will dedicate senior / experienced resources to your project and that most of the work will not be delegated to junior team members.

Another factor to consider is to ensure you are not at a disadvantage when you are negotiating with a seasoned business acquirer. Be candid with yourself about your skills and appetite to run this process. A career spent as an entrepreneur may not prepare you to deal directly with a financial buyer particularly when the topic for discussion is something that you may have invested a lifetime building and to which you have a strong emotional attachment.

Selling your business could truly be one of the most stressful and emotional experiences of your business life – but it does not have to be. To make the experience run smoothly there are several factors that can be addressed in advance of a transaction. The items outlined below are our opinion on some of the best ways to prepare your business for sale and maximize the value once you sell.

- Ensure the future financial stability and value of the business.
- Reduce the potential tax liabilities of transferring the ownership.
- Set a timetable for transfer of ownership to the successor, whether a family member, employee or an outside purchaser.
- Contribute to the growth of the business in terms of market share, profitability and size.
- Provide stability for employees.

The downside of not planning is undeniable: unprepared owners will be forced to sell at a discount with the associated risk of business closure and loss of jobs.[8]

Selling your business will be a lengthy process even under the best circumstances. A rough rule of thumb is that it can take up to one year to prepare the business prior to putting it on market, one year until the deal is completed and a further year to fully exit from day to day operations. Therefore, if you are considering selling your business with the goal of being out in three years, the best time to start the process is today.

Rather than go through the process of a sale to a third party, owners often consider a transfer of the business to the next generation. Our view is that while this might make sense for some businesses, more often this is not generally the best solution for the sustainability of the business. In our experience only roughly one third of family businesses survive from the first generation into the second, while perhaps only half that number survive into the third generation.[9]

Selling your business has some parallels to selling your house… you must ensure that your business shows well. Make sure the office and shop are clean and organized, a disorganized or messy business is a red-flag to investors as it raises the concerns there could be "messes" elsewhere in the business, like the financial statements. Basically what you are attempting to do is to make the business easy to buy… have in place detailed operating manuals and procedures as well as a second tier of management that will make the transition for new owners a smooth one. The last thing you want is for a potential purchaser to believe that once you leave, so will the business.

It is also necessary to understand how your business' performance compares to other businesses in the same or similar industries. Buyers often hear claims *"my business is a best in class performer"* or *"we are a top-quartile company"* and they usually are skeptical. Ensure that before you present your business for sale that you do in fact know how your business stacks up from both a profitability and balance sheet perspective versus other companies in your industry because astute business purchasers will certainly have that information. If you make the above noted claims, have the ability to back them up.

CHAPTER 4

Valuing Your Business – Overview

The competitor to be feared is one who never bothers about you at all, but goes on making his own business better all the time.

– Henry Ford

A t the most basic level there are three components required for determining the value of any business regardless of industry, sector, type, business model, structure or size. The three components are sustainable cash flow, required rate of return and the company's balance sheet or asset package. Each of these components are interconnected and through the analysis of each component a valuation of a business can be completed.

Sustainable cash flow

When a business is purchased a great deal of work goes into understanding the company's historical and projected cash flows and profits. The purchaser is effectively buying the future cash flows that the business will generate to the benefit of its stakeholders, hence maximum emphasis is placed on understanding, and determining, a reasonable expectation of the company's sustainable (future) cash flows. Simply put, in a going concern business, key to any valuation is expected future cash flows.

Required rate of return

The second element of a business valuation is "the rate of return expectation". Once an estimate of future cash flows have been determined, one has to assess the required rate of return to be earned on those cash flows corresponding to the risk profile associated with that cash flow stream. The higher the risk of the estimated future cash flows not being realized, the higher rate of return that will be required by the purchaser. Put another way, safer investments (e.g. government bonds) have lower required returns as compared with riskier investments (e.g. junk bonds).

Balance sheet or asset package

The third component of any valuation is determining what kind of "balance sheet or asset package", including amount of working capital and capital assets, is required to be in place to earn/generate the future cash flow stream at the expected or required rate of return. In simple terms think of this as the physical building blocks of your business. Together these three interconnected components formulate the value of any business and are presented as the following questions guide the process:

1. What are the future cash flows this business will generate?
2. What is the risk profile and corresponding required rate of return these cash flows will generate?
3. What type of balance sheet is required to generate the cash flow stream which will result in the required rate of return?

The following section will elaborate on each of the above value components to help you understand the business valuation process in the context of your business.

There is little success where there is little laughter.

– Andrew Carnegie

CHAPTER 5

Valuing Your Business – Cash is King

I do not believe a man can ever leave his business. He ought to think of it by day and dream of it by night.

– Henry Ford

C ash flows are the first component of value. In this chapter we will review both Discretionary After Tax Cash Flow and Earnings Before Interest Taxes Depreciation and Amortization ("EBITDA").

Why is cash flow important? "Cash is King" – you will undoubtedly have heard this expression before, but in the case of business valuation there is no more true a statement. Financial statements are prepared according to specified accounting policies such as GAAP, ASPE or IFRS and while a company's net income is an important measure of performance, cash flow is equally as important if not more important. To be clear, net income is not cash flow. Numerous adjustments are required to be made to net income to derive a company's cash flow. The specific adjustments required are beyond this book, however it is important to highlight the reason that cash flow is so important. Cash flow pays the interest on debt, cash flow pays the taxes, pays owner dividends or bonuses at year-end, cash flow is required to make investments in capital assets and cash is required to take advantage of growth opportunities.

There are really two derivatives of earnings that correspond to cash flow that are used in valuing businesses. The first is discretionary after tax cash flow. This is cash that is generated in the business that is available for either distribution to the shareholders or to invest in further growth opportunities (e.g. purchase of new machinery or building expansion). It is discretionary because the business owner can do with it whatever they want without jeopardizing the current steady-state performance of the business. It is discretionary because it is the cash that is generated after paying the debt servicing costs, the income tax owed in the year, employee bonuses, and ultimately creates the return on the invested equity capital in the business.

Discretionary after tax cash flow is the pure form of cash flow a business generates and is fundamentally the best cash flow stream to use when valuing a business.

EBITDA

The second form of cash flow that is more commonly used in valuations is EBITDA.

EBITDA is a term used so frequently and under so many, often varying, circumstances that we often question whether, beyond what the letters stand for, people have a clear idea of its meaning. EBITDA stands for Earnings Before Interest Taxes Depreciation and Amortization, but its true utility is as an estimate or proxy of cash flow.

EBITDA is used to standardize financial results so as to eliminate the impact of business decisions of the existing corporate management with respect to a company's capital structure, the impact of tax structure, the state of the capital assets and the attendant depreciation policy implementation. More simply put, EBITDA allows an investor to quickly compare and analyze different businesses in a consistent manner. When the items above are "added back" what remains is a number that represents the amount that would be available to all stakeholders – the shareholders, the lenders and the government.

EBITDA does however have its limitations, including, amongst others, that there is no allowance for ongoing capital expenditure. All things being equal, a business with annual require capital expenditures of $500,000 is different from a business with annual capital expenditure requirement of $250,000. In Warren Buffet's 2000 letter to shareholders, he refers to management that mention only EBITDA instead of Net Income:

> "References to EBITDA make us shudder - does management think that the tooth fairy pays for capital expenditures?"

At the risk of trying to paraphrase an investing legend, what Buffet is saying is that by overlooking the depreciation expense (or capital expenditure requirements) a business (or acquirer) is at risk of making faulty decisions. Therefore, while EBITDA is used as a tool to compare similar businesses, in isolation it only tells part of the story. For instance, EBITDA margin (% EBITDA compared to Revenue) of two similar businesses shows the quality of one company to the other that a focus on absolute EBITDA levels would miss. The table below illustrates two similar businesses with dramatically different operating results. While both businesses have $2.3 million in EBITDA, all other things being equal Zenith Manufacturing has better EBITDA margins.

		Company 1	Zenith Manufacturing
Revenue	a	$21,000,000	$16,000,000
Net Income		$1,600,000	$1,600,000
add: Income taxes		$400,000	$400,000
add: interest in long term debt		$200,000	$200,000
add: depreciation and amortization		$100,000	$100,000
EBITDA	b	$ 2,300,000	$2,300,000
EBITDA margin	b/a	11.0%	14.4%

Clearly while both companies have the same EBITDA, Zenith Manufacturing, with higher EBITDA margins, has higher quality earnings. Therefore, Zenith would be better positioned to weather more severe business downturns and would be able to reinvest more back into the business to capitalize on growth opportunities.

Is EBITDA growing, steady or declining year over year? The trends in any business are more important than the results of any one single year in isolation. When a business is analyzed, the past several years' results are considered to determine the level of sustainable EBITDA of the business. If EBITDA is steadily increasing, as a result of investment in capital assets and general expansion of the business, then this represents a positive EBITDA trend. On the other hand if a business has erratic EBITDA results over the last few years and in the most recent year posts its best ever results, the level of sustainable EBITDA would be questioned.

Why is EBITDA used? EBITDA is used to make the business valuation process simpler for acquirers when they get a first look at a new opportunity. Though when the time comes to make a detailed assessment or valuation of the business, usually the items excluded in calculating EBITDA are reconsidered and diligently scrutinized. What this means for a business owner is that while it may be important to know what their company's EBITDA is, it is much more important to focus on ensuring:

- Trend: positive and stable,

- Margins: stable, if not improving,

- Composition: EBITDA (depreciation, interest and taxes) is calculated in a prudent manner, and

- CAPEX: produces sustainable growth in the business.

EBITDA Multiple

As a business owner you have most likely heard someone refer to an 'EBITDA multiple'. At the core an EBITDA multiple is exactly like it sounds. However, this is more complicated than just assuming that the typical multiple is 4 times. Firstly, a multiple is simply the inverse of the rate of return that an investment in a business should return to the stakeholders. If the rate of return expectation over the long term is 25%, then 1 divided by 25% equals 4; therefore the multiple is 4x.

As discussed above, EBITDA represents cash flow available to all stakeholders in the business, most notably, business owners and lenders. Therefore, the multiple on these cash flows should correspond to their respective expected rates of return on the capital that they have invested in the business.

A cash flow multiple must be matched appropriately to the appropriate income stream. Meaning if you are using a pre-tax income stream the multiple should be based on a pre-tax rate of return. Similarly, if the income stream is available only to the shareholders after paying out all taxes and interest costs, the multiple should be one that includes the rate of return for shareholders on an after tax basis. There are several technical components involved in calculating an EBITDA multiple:

- Equity rate of return
- Interest rate on debt
- Appropriate capital structure (percentage of debt and equity or debt to equity ratio)
- Expected sustainable growth rate for EBITDA
- Capital expenditures as a percentage of EBITDA

Equity rate of return is calculated using a build-up approach, meaning we start with a risk free rate of return (e.g. Government of Canada bond) of say 5%. To that we add risk premiums, as the risk profile of the investment increases. For example:

Risk free rate - long Canada bonds	5%
Add: Public market equity risk premium	5%
Add: Public market small/micro cap size premium	5%
Add: Company specific factors	5%
Add: Liquidity premium for privately held equity investment	5%
After tax rate of return on Equity	25%
Tax rate	30%
Pre-tax rate of return on Equity	36%

- For the interest rate on long-term debt we will assume a blended rate of 10% for all long-term debt (conventional term and sub debt).

- As for the appropriate capital structure we can assume a debt to equity ratio of 1 to 2, which corresponds to debt of 33% and equity of 66%.

- Expected sustainable growth rate for EBITDA of 5%.

- Capital expenditures as a percentage of EBITDA of 10% - meaning that if EBITDA is $2 million, capital expenditures to support current operations and growth of 5% (above) is approximately $200,000 per year.

Using these components, the EBITDA multiple is calculated as follows:

Pre-tax return on equity	C	36%
Debt rate	D	10%
Growth rate	G	-5%
Appropriate amount of debt per leverage analysis:	E	33%
Value of levered equity	F	67%
WACC = ((E/(E+F)*D)+((1-E/(E+F))*C) + G	WACC	22%
EBITDA before CAPEX Multiple	G	4.5
CAPEX as a % of EBITDA	1/WACC = F	10%
EBITDA multiple - after CAPEX	F-G = Net EBITDA Multiple	4.0

In summary, the illustration above is the detailed way to determine an EBITDA multiple. When someone tells you they got a 4 x EBITDA for their business, you will understand what it means.

Now that the EBITDA multiple mystery is untangled, the more pressing question business owners ask is *"What kind of EBITDA multiple would a company like mine get?"*

EBITDA multiples are often discussed loosely and can depend on what EBITDA is used and how EBITDA is positioned when selling. Is the valuation based on a 12 month trailing basis, weighted average, forecast results, or a combination of historical and forecasted results? Is the working capital surplus included and what other normalizations to EBITDA are reflected?

Consider the following example of Rogers Technology with the following EBITDA profile.

Rogers Technology Inc.						
Company A	3 years ago	2 years ago	Last year	Current year	TTM	Forecast next year
EBITDA	$1.8 mil	$2.1 mil	$2.0 mil	$2.3 mil	$2.2 mil	$2.3 mil

As illustrated in Scenario A, a 4x EBITDA multiple results in dramatically different results depending on what EBITDA is being discussed. Where is this table?

Rogers Technology Inc.			
	EBITDA	Multiple	Enterprise Value
Simple 4 year Average	$2.0 mil	4.4 x	$9.0 mil
Weighted Average	$2.1 mil	4.3 x	$9.0 mil
Most recent fiscal year	$2.3 mil	4.0 x	$9.0 mil
Trailing 12 months	$2.2 mil	4.1 x	$9.0 mil
Forecast	$2.3 mil	3.9 x	$9.0 mil

Furthermore, the above table shows that the EBITDA multiple can be significantly different when discussing the same purchase price. The level of EBITDA multiple a business attracts in the marketplace when the time comes to sell is based on a number of factors, some of which include:

- Economic outlook and forecast
- Quality of the management team
- Competitiveness of the industry
- Balance sheet condition
- Historical growth profile
- Consistency of track record

The point we are trying to make here is that EBITDA is not a definitive term or precise quantity and understanding how buyers of your business may use it is an important part of the sale process. Furthermore many factors can impact what EBITDA is used in determining value.

To be successful, you have to have your heart in your business and your business in your heart.

– Thomas J. Watson

CHAPTER 6

Valuing Your Business – Normalization Adjustments

You have to learn the rules of the game. And then you have to play better than anyone else.

– *Albert Einstein*

What are normalizations to cash flow (or EBITDA)? Business owners generally know that while their financial statements may be prepared according to accounting rules they do not always provide the most useful information, particularly when it comes to providing insight into the value of their business. Furthermore, many business owners think that because their financial statements are audited or reviewed by a chartered accountant that they are "clean". While they may be "clean" for financial reporting purposes to the bank, for valuation purposes, a different definition of "clean" is used.

When calculating the sustainable or recurring cash flows of a business there are many aspects that must be taken into consideration to determine what is the cash flow. Expenses may be added to and subtracted from the cash flow to arrive at the adjusted operational cash flows. For example, items that have been expensed and are not part of true operational expenses of the business should be added back to determine the adjusted cash flow. Conversely, expenses that have not been accounted for which are true operational expenses should be subtracted from the cash flow.

Examples of normalizations that would increase recurring cash flow:

- If the shareholders of the company paid out management fees to themselves each year, which are in excess of what the fair market salary would be, the excess amount of a manager's salary should be normalized, adding to the cash flow. The test for determining the amount of the adjustment is to determine what it would cost to hire a manager or executive to replace the owner. If the fair market compensation is $200,000, anything paid to the owner in excess of this amount would represent an adjustment to cash flow.

- If the company was involved in a lawsuit and paid legal costs for the litigation, 100% of these costs would be considered non-operational and, assuming lawsuits are not a normal occurrence, should be normalized, adding to the recurring cash flow.

- Expenses generated by redundant assets – For example the business owns a vacation property for the owner and pays the maintenance costs on this property. The property is a redundant asset and the costs can be added back to cash flow.

- Rent of facilities at above market rent. Many businesses do not own their facilities but rather lease them from the business owner. The rent is often arbitrarily set above market rents and the difference can be added back to cash flow.

Examples of normalizations that would decrease cash flow:

- It is not uncommon for the principals in the business to own the core real-estate and to rent that real-estate to the business at below market rates. In the event that this takes place, cash flow must be normalized to account for fair market rates of the analysis period.

- No salary for management – management compensation below market

- R&D expenses

- Insufficient provisioning for warranty expense

- Insufficient provisioning for bad debt expense

- Out of period adjustments

- Significant accrual to actual differences

- Owners' benefits such as personal term, whole life insurance, key man insurance, also pension or RRSP contributions paid by the company

You may ask how do normalizations impact the value of my business? Normalizations are very important in every valuation as the impact on cash flow is ultimately impacted by a multiple. For instance, in the example below, normalizations of $445,000 could result in $1.78

million of incremental value using a 4x multiple based on trailing year's EBITDA.

		Randall Packaging
EBITDA	a	$2,000,000
EBITDA Multiple	b	4.0 x
Enterprise Value	a x b = c	$8,000,000
Normalizations:		
Excess Management Fees	e	$500,000
One Time Legal Cost	f	$125,000
Below Market Rent	g	($180,000)
Total Normalizations	e+f+g = h	$445,000
Normalized EBITDA	a+h = i	$2,445,000
EBITDA Multiple	b	4.0 x
Enterprise Value	i x b = j	$9,780,000
INCREMENTAL VALUE	j-c	$1,780,000

While it is important to present adjustments to normalize cash flows, if so warranted, too many adjustments may be viewed negatively by a purchaser. Similarly, superficial or arguable adjustments may diminish or render moot legitimate adjustments. An abundance of adjustments resulting in significantly adjusted income statement may also lead to the conclusion that the company was run as the owner's personal piggy bank and not as a professionally managed business. While important to consider and reflect significant or key adjustments, as a general rule, the fewer adjustments to reported financial statements, the better.

How your business is positioned and marketed is as important to the ultimate sale outcome as the quality of the business itself.

– *Equicapita*

CHAPTER 7

Valuing Your Business – Forecast

People are definitely a company's greatest asset. It doesn't make any difference whether the product is cars or cosmetics. A company is only as good as the people it keeps.

– Mary Kay Ash

At this point you may be asking yourself, if it is all about future cash flows, shouldn't I show a huge growth forecast? If the future cash flows of the business are one of the keys to determining value, then it makes sense that the forecast should be presented in a manner that shows dramatic growth as in the graph below.

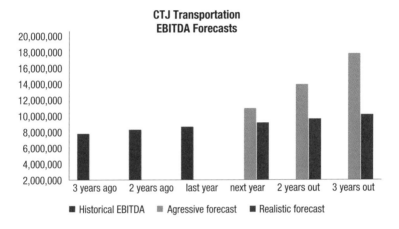

CTJ Transportation has had a very impressive track record of consistent EBITDA growth, though the growth has been typically in the range of between 5% and 10% annually. The aggressive forecast shows growth profiles at approximately 33% for next 3 years and EBITDA at levels never even approached by the company before. When forecasts like these are put forward as the company's future prospects there are two problems that arise. The first is the question of integrity of management, whether or not the vendors are actually dealing in good faith. The second problem is that even if management insists the forecast is real, since a transaction generally evolves over a period of several months if the business is not tracking to achieve the forecast, the purchaser may begin to lose confidence in management resulting in either a request for a purchase price revision or the purchaser walking away altogether.

If you are looking to get paid on forecasted earnings, the best scenario is to put forward a well thought out, fully supported forecast that although may be optimistic, it is still obtainable for the company. In the graph above it is shown as the "realistic forecast" that reflects 8% growth over each of the next of three years, which is relatively consistent with the growth profile for the past three years. To forecast more will result likely result in the forecast being discounted significantly by potential purchasers and will generally result in reduced offer prices for the business.

Plans are nothing; planning is everything.

– Dwight D. Eisenhower

CHAPTER 8

Valuing Your Business – Goodwill

Ego stops you from getting things done and getting people to work with you. That's why I firmly believe that ego and success are not compatible.

– Harvey Mackay

What is goodwill? Doesn't every business have it? One of the biggest misconceptions about goodwill is that every business owner thinks his or her business has enormous goodwill; meaning they typically think that their business is worth a great deal more than it is.

Often this stems from the belief that goodwill is generated by the length of time a business has been around. The term goodwill is often casually applied in situations where it is really not applicable. The technical definition of goodwill is *'the value of a business attributable to the excess earnings that a business generates over and above that which would be expected to be generated on the net equity in the business'*.

The table below gives a sample illustration how goodwill can be calculated. We will group all intangible assets together with goodwill to determine the aggregate value and refer to it as goodwill. In this example, we have used the excess earnings model – which assumes an investor or business owner would expect to earn a risk adjusted rate of return on the tangible equity in the business of approximately 3 times the risk free bond rate, or 13%. This would translate into earnings of approximately $390,000.

The remaining earnings would be attributable to goodwill, meaning the things that the business does differently than its competitors that translate into higher returns for the shareholders or hidden assets in the business that contribute to higher earnings.

To determine the value of the goodwill one has to look at the expected rate of return an owner or investor would expect to earn, consistently, on the group of intangible assets if one were to own the business. In this example we have used three times the rate expected on the tangible net worth or 39%. The reason the expected rate of return is so much higher on intangibles is that there is nothing to fall back on or to recover if those earnings start to decline or disappear, unlike on tangible assets that can always be sold or auctioned.

Reserve Fluids Inc. Excess Earnings Valuation Indicator		
Tangible Net Worth ("TNW")	a	$6,500,000
Expected Return on Tangible Net Worth	b	13.00%
(3 times risk free rate)		
Profit Attributable To Tangible Net Worth	a*b=c	$845,000
Maintainable Pre-Tax Profit/EBITDA	d	$3,000,000
Less: Profit Attributable to Net Worth	c	($845,000)
Profit Attributable to Goodwill (& other intanbibles)	d-c=e	$2,155,000
Expected Rate of Return on Goodwill	f	39.00%
3.0 times rate on TNW		
Value of Goodwill	e/f=g	$5,500,000
Add: TNW	a	$6,500,000
Implied Value of Business	g+a=v	$12,000,000
Expected Multiple of EBITDA	v/u	4.00
Note: Maintainable EBITDA	u	$3,000,000

CHAPTER 9

Valuing Your Business – Balance Sheet

If you think you can do a thing or think you can't do a thing, you're right.

– Henry Ford

How does my balance sheet translate into business value? The balance sheet, is often the most overlooked component of a business' value, but no less important than all the others. Without a balance sheet – cash flow from a business would not be possible. In essence, the balance sheet, or package of assets, liabilities and equity is the essential component of the business, and unless it is structured in an appropriate way a business will be in jeopardy. For this section we will we will focus on Equitable Manufacturing's balance sheet as profiled on the following page, to see how it stacks up compared to its peers and assess its impact on corporate value.

It is only when one starts to take apart the balance sheet does it really begin to tell the story. We analyze a balance sheet based on four main factors, focusing our attention on liquidity, profitability, activity and capital structure ratios.

- Composition of current assets – how liquid are the assets. Current implies the ability to turn into cash within one year.

- The ratio of current assets over current liabilities – or how much working capital the business actually has to pursue growth versus simply meet ongoing obligations. We typically assess this based on an operational review, instead of simply basing it on GAAP accounting treatments.

- The composition of liabilities – current vs. long term, third party vs. related party, amortization period, nature of the debt – callable or term.

- The capacity for new debt – how much debt the company could take on if new opportunities were presented, balanced with the ratio of total debt to tangible net worth of the business – according to standards in the industry and comparison to peers.

Balance Sheet		
Assets		
Cash & Equivalents		$294,021
Trade Receivables (net)		$1,866,800
Inventory		$1,166,750
All Other Current Assets		$70,005
	Total Current Assets	3,397,576
Fixed Assets (net)		$672,000
Intangible Assets		$84,000
All Other Non-Current Assets		$513,424
	Total	$4,667,000
Liabilities		
Trade Payables		$1,400,050
Notes Payable - Short Term		$728,052
Current Maturity L/T/D		$233,350
Income Taxes Payable		$14,001
All Other Current Liabilities		$233,350
	Total Current Liabilities	$2,608,803
Long-Term Debt		$326,690
Deferred Taxes		$9,334
All Other Non-Current Debt		$238,017
	Total	$3,182,844
Equity		
Equity		$1,184,156
	Total Liabilities & Equity	$4,667,000

Equitable Manufacturing's balance sheet has $4.6 million in assets – based on the parameters above – it has approximately $1.9 million in accounts receivable out of $3.4 million of total current assets. However, the real problem lies in the fact that they only have net working capital of less than $700,000 on sales of $14 million. The company is getting tight with its liquidity and they should stay on top of working capital before it gets too tight. Tightness in working capital may be due in part to the fact that they have experienced rapid growth and have financed long-term assets for growth (new capital assets) with short term financing, which has facilitated growth – but has hampered flexibility.

What is a "required equity injection" or "excess leverage"? When one is reviewing a balance sheet and assesses that there is too much debt compared to industry standards or even to prudent debt levels, it will likely be stated that the company requires an equity injection to continue successful operations. In a valuation context, this corresponds to a dollar for dollar increase in the value of the business.

Should I clean up my balance sheet before I sell? We are often asked if a balance sheet should be cleaned up before the sale process begins. The easy answer of course is "yes". However sometimes it may be unduly complicated to strip out assets prior to a transaction. Part of the problem lies in the fact that if there is any bank debt in the company, a release will be required from the bank to remove assets that are used as collateral under the general security agreement. Just as important as stripping out the assets, is identifying these excess assets in advance of a transaction so they can be easily explained as assets that will be retained by the selling ownership group. If a business owner wishes to sell some or all of the excess assets with the business, these would be valued independently of the business so it would be necessary to establish fair market value for the items.

Truth is a tendency.
– Buckminster Fuller

Research indicates that employees have three prime needs: Interesting work, recognition for doing a good job, and being let in on things that are going on in the company.

– Zig Ziglar

CHAPTER 10

Valuing Your Business – Working Capital

The difference between a successful person and others is not a lack of strength, not a lack of knowledge, but rather a lack of will.

– *Vince Lombardi*

How does working capital impact the value of my business? Firstly, an overriding principle of valuation, particularly in valuing operational going concern businesses, is that working capital is included in the business. Working capital is typically a contentious issue over the course of a transaction as the vendor and the purchaser will often have divergent views as to what the business requires. Also, working capital is also often misunderstood. Ultimately working capital will fall into one of three categories and as the vendor you must be ready to deal with the results:

- Sufficient / appropriate / adequate
- Surplus / excess
- Deficient / shortfall

The real question is how much working capital is required for this business to continue operating as it is now and to follow the stated growth trajectory? What is the level of working capital that is commensurate with earnings? Working capital levels are assessed to determine where a company sits. Working capital levels are measured against industry norms, typical banking covenant ratios, percentage of forecast sales, and requirements based on financial and operational forecasts.

Sufficient working capital levels are usually shown as amounts that have been consistently retained in the business, year after year, while allowing for distributions to shareholders for bonuses or dividends that have not been required to be re-loaned to the business as shareholder loans. What this means is that often a business owner receives an annual shareholder bonus to reduce the taxable income of the company, the company pays the tax on the lower income, the shareholder pays the tax on income received and then the shareholder loans the money back to the business to fund operations, and this often occurs year after year.

This is an example of a shareholder financing a company's ongoing operations and shows that the shareholder loan capital is required for the ongoing operations of the business. If the annual distribution is paid out of the company and doesn't come back in as a shareholder loan, this shows that the company is operating form its own resources and can actually distribute the discretionary cash flow.

Deficient working capital levels are characterized in two ways. The first is where there are more current liabilities than current assets and the company will have ongoing difficulty meeting its obligations. The second and less obvious, is where a company still has a positive working capital balance, but the amount of working capital is insufficient to take on new initiatives, support growth and generally requires the business to adopt the status quo.

What is considered a surplus working capital position and how can this be justified?   Adequate working capital is the working capital to run the business in a sustained state, not considering growth.   If the EBITDA that is being used in a multiple approach incorporates forecasted growth in EBITDA, then the amount of working capital should be sufficient to handle the growth profile which would be a higher requirement and may reduce perceived working capital surplus.

Every business is different and some of the items that should be considered in the determination of working capital surplus/deficiency are the following:

- Comparison to industry norms for top performing companies
- Revenue to working capital ratios
- Seasonality
- Growth capital expenditure requirements
- Inventory turns

- A/R days

- A/P days

- Maximum amount of operating line of credit or cash available

- If surplus working capital is being used to gain purchasing discounts

Set out below are examples of two companies that at first glance appear identical from a revenue and EBITDA perspective. However, when working capital is analyzed, Caliber Diversified Industries has much greater requirements than its erstwhile peer.

Caliber Diversified Industries:

- Caliber has a current ratio of 1.78 and a working capital balance of approximately $1.5 Million. Next year's sales are forecast at $15 million.

- $2.2 million EBITDA x 4.0X Multiple = $8.8 million Entity Value.

- Working Capital of $1.5 million of which is $500,000 is considered a working capital surplus and therefore is added to the purchase price.

- $8.8 million Entity Value plus $500,000 excess working capital = $9.3 Million value.

- $9.3 Million Entity Value / $2.2 million EBITDA = 4.23x EBITDA multiple.

Company 2:

- $2.2 million EBITDA x 4X Multiple = $8.8 million Entity Value.

- Working Capital of $600,000 that is considered insufficient for normal operations by $400,000, and is deducted from the purchase price, to result in a $8.2 Million purchase price.

- $8.2 Million value/ $2.2 million EBITDA = 3.73x EBITDA multiple.

By correctly positioning Caliber to the purchaser, the vendor in this situation receives the equivalent of a 10% higher EBITDA multiple. As illustrated, if working capital is not positioned properly, a business owner may sell his business at a discount not even realizing he is leaving money on the table. The astute business purchaser would not like to pay for excess working capital and views this as a discount to the purchase price. It is in the best interest of the purchaser to not make the vendor aware of any surplus working capital that may be included in the negotiated purchase price.

An economist's guess is liable to be as good as anybody else's.

— Will Rogers

CHAPTER 11

Valuing Your Business – Capital Expenditures ("Capex")

There are no secrets to success. It is the result of preparation, hard work, and learning from failure.

– *Colin Powell*

Capital expenditures – How do they effect growth and stable earnings? Most businesses would expect to see relatively consistent annual capital expenditures. On the other hand, a company that is growing or has growth plans would typically have capital expenditures that are greater than the average depreciation expense. This shows investment in the business over and above the norm. We often see businesses with stated growth plans that are rather aggressive, but are not matched with corresponding historical or planned increases in capital expenditures. This shows that the company is just hoping for growth instead of truly creating it. Capital expenditures can impact value in two key ways. If ongoing maintenance capital expenditures are consistent and represent a significant component of otherwise "discretionary" cash flow, this shows a relatively capital intensive business or a business with a slate of older assets that need replacing, and cash flows would be adjusted to show the ongoing nature of these cash outflows. This would reduce the value compared to a business that is not capital intensive or has a newer group of assets with a longer life and a delayed requirement for additional investment. If on the other hand the capital expenditures are fairly lumpy and are followed by periods of growth, this shows a business that is building capacity and although capital expenditures would be considered in forecasting future cash flows, future cash flows would reflect a growth profile because of the consistent investment in additional capacity.

Remember, ultimately it is a metric known as Free Cash Flow ("FCF") that buyers are looking for in your business - FCF is the measure of how much cash a business generates after accounting for capital expenditures such as buildings or equipment and is the cash that can be used for expansion, dividends, reducing debt, or other purposes. Therefore, while profitability is one measure of the value of the business, FCF is ultimately just as important. In simple terms know the difference in your business between the Capex that is require to maintain current profitability and the Capex required for any projected growth.

Small businesses are the backbone of our communities.

— *Tom Allen*

CHAPTER 12

Valuing Your Business – Redundant Assets

If you work just for money, you'll never make it, but if you love what you're doing and you always put the customer first, success will be yours.

— *Ray Kroc*

What are "redundant assets"? Redundant assets are assets that are included on the balance sheet (owned by the company) but are not required for the ongoing operations of the business. Some examples of redundant assets are:

- Marketable securities held by the company in a brokerage account
- Corporate retreat or vacation home
- The land and building that the company operates from (discussed in a later chapter)
- Cash surrender values of life insurance policies
- Golf course membership
- Cash

As in the case of Equitable Manufacturing, the company has cash and equivalents sitting on the balance sheet of approximately $300,000 (See Equitable Manufacturing balance sheet on page 54). Also included in other non-current assets is the company owned retreat in Palm Springs, California, recently appraised at $500,000. We would consider these items as redundant assets in assessing the value of the business, in concert with an assessment of the working capital (above) whereby we determined that the company has surplus working capital of $1.5 million. Furthermore the company owns its land and buildings. We will also consider these redundant assets because if the company did not own them they could simply lease same or similar facilities to operate from.

The reason these items are considered redundant or excess is that because if any of them were removed from the business, the business results would not be unduly impacted and should the business be sold, these assets these assets would not likely be included in a business transaction.

Industry is fortune's right hand, and frugality its left.

– *John Ray*

CHAPTER 13

Valuing Your Business – Real Estate

Capital isn't that important in business. Experience isn't that important. You can get both of these things. What is important is ideas.

– *Harvey S. Firestone*

What does my real estate have to with the value of my business? Corporate owned real estate has more to do with a business owner's overall wealth than it does to the value of the business. Many business owners we deal with also own the commercial real estate from which their businesses operate. Generally, business owners seem to be in tune with the value of their real estate holdings, but not necessarily how the real estate can impact the value of their business.

Sophisticated purchasers will attempt to purchase the business and real estate from a business owner and proclaim that the business requires the premises to continue operations so they should be sold together as a package. While that may be true, it is extremely important to value each asset separately – the business as one asset and the real estate as the second asset.

Consider the case of Inland Metal Inc. in the following example, as a business that owns their real estate and how the different treatment can result in two dramatically different levels of proceeds to the owner.

Inland Metal Inc.		
	Scenario A Business and Real Estate together	**Scenario B** Business and Real Estate as separate assets
Business A	rent not deducted from EBITDA	rent deducted from EBITDA
Gross EBITDA	$2.0 million	$2.0 million
Less: Market level rent		-$0.2 million
Adjusted EBITDA	$2.0 million	$1.8 million
EBITDA Multiple	4.0 x	4.0 x
Enterprise value	$8.0 million	$7.2 million
Market level rent		$0.2 million
Real Estate Cap. Rate		8%
Real estate value	included above	$2.5 million
Total proceeds	$8.0 million	$9.7 million

As shown in Scenario B, deducting rent payments from EBITDA may seem counter intuitive but you will note that it results in greater proceeds to the business owner.

The simple reason is that commercial real estate is seen as a lower risk profile asset than an operating business. The reason is that all commercial real estate needs for it to generate a return on investment is a tenant in place that is reliably paying rent in the short term and that is expected to be in place for the long term. As a result, there is a consistent spread between real estate multiples and business multiples, reflecting the differing risk profiles of each asset.

Although Equicapita does not acquire real-estate for its investment portfolio we do have relationships with funds that specialize in this and we are always willing to discuss a proposal where the real-state and/or the business you own is part of a transaction.

Doubt is not a pleasant condition, but certainty is absurd.

– Voltaire

CHAPTER 14

Pursue a Growth Strategy

Just because
something doesn't do
what you planned it
to do doesn't mean
it's useless.

— Thomas A. Edison

The option referenced in Chapter 2 of "Have someone run it in your place" really corresponds to a transition of the business either in whole or in part relating to a succession plan with the ultimate goal of realizing in the value you have created. A succession plan implies that you either have people within the organization or within the industry transition in to leadership roles within your company. These types of transactions include management buy-out ("MBO"), management buy-in ("MBI").

A MBO transaction is typically an option that a business owner will consider when the business owner has established a strong management team. Furthermore that management team has expressed a keen interest in owning the business and have capital resources at their disposal to support such a transaction. In order for a MBO transaction to be completed the management team requires its own capital along with the support of a financial sponsor (Private equity firm), bank financing and usually some element of vendor financing.

A MBI transaction is similar in nature to a MBO transaction except some or all of the management involved with the transaction come from outside of the business. The management for an MBI are often from within the industry (competitor, customer or supplier) and have a strong knowledge of the business and industry and usually have an established relationship with the business owner and/or some of the other management within the business.

A typical transaction structure for a MBO/MBI transaction is illustrated using

Excelsior Services Ltd. MBO/MBI Transaction Structure			
		Transaction	
EBITDA		$2.5 million	
EBITDA Multiple		4.0 x	
Enterprise value		$10.0 million	
Source of Financing	multiple of EBITDA	Amount of financing	
Management Equity	0.5x	$1.25 million	$1.25 million
Conventional bank debt	~1 x	$2.50 million	$2.50 million
Mezzanine financing	~1 to 2 x	$2.50 million	$5.00 million
Vendor financing	remainder	$3.75 million	$1.25 million
		$10.00 million	$10.00 million

Of note, Equicapita has relationships with funds that provide
capital to facilitate MBO and MBI transactions.

Coming together is a beginning; keeping together is progress; working together is success.

– Henry Ford

CHAPTER 15

Have Someone Run Your Business - Succession Planning

The measure of success is not whether you have a tough problem to deal with, but whether it is the same problem you had last year.

– *John Foster Dulles*

The option referenced in Chapter 2 of "Pursue a growth strategy" corresponds to bringing on a partner or obtaining additional capital to facilitate growth. This type of transaction can involve selling a component of the business (say 20%) where the capital comes in to support growth initiatives or taking on a form of debt (or quasi-debt or quasi-equity ie. Mezzanine financing) to support growth initiatives. These strategies are typically pursued in an effort to grow a business so that the additional time, effort and risk involved in the strategy is sufficiently offset by the expectation that the ultimate exit or sale transaction is at a substantially higher value such that is than would have been the realized value had the growth strategy not been pursued.

Outlined below are the potential different outcomes of bringing on growth financing compared to simply selling your business as it currently exists, provided of course it is a saleable business.

Inland Metal Inc.				
	Scenario A Business under current ownership	Scenario B Business with mezz financing		Scenario C Business with growth partner
Gross EBITDA	$2.5 million	$3.5 million		$3.5 million
EBITDA Multiple	4.0 x	4.0 x		4.0 x
Enterprise value	$10.0 million	$14.0 million		$14.0 million
Mezzanine financing repayment		$2.0 million		
Minority Equity Partner Repayment			20%	$2.8 million
Residual Equity Value - Original Owner	$10.0 million	$12.0 million		$11.2 million
Benefit of Growth Strategy	-	$2.0 million		$1.2 million

Of note, Equicapita has relationships with funds that provide growth capital in the form of mezzanine financing.

In the business world,
the rearview mirror is
always clearer than
the windshield.

– *Warren Buffett*

CHAPTER 16

Improving Saleability

Each player must accept the cards life deals him or her: but once they are in hand, he or she alone must decide how to play the cards in order to win the game.

— *Voltaire*

There are several factors that contribute to the "saleability" of any business. In this chapter we outline important factors that contribute to higher business values in a transaction environment. We boil it down to some key areas that are directly controllable by the business owner and management team. The overriding message in this section is that for a business that took many years to build and which has significant value locked up, it is well worth the effort to enhance your "saleability" and ultimately the value received.

If you assume the value of your business is $5 million today, by working through the key areas over the period of a year the value could be increased substantially and the business could sell in a much shorter period of time.

Sustainable competitive advantage is always something that buyers will want to understand – particularly whether your business has one. What this really means is that if a business is in a competitive industry, it possesses some type of competitive obstacle that is defendable – similar to a moat around a castle. There is no way to attack a castle without crossing the moat – well the same can be said for a sustainable competitive advantage. A competitive advantage that cannot be readily copied by competitors enhances the value of your business.

Typically sustainable competitive advantages result from superior skills and superior resources[10]. Superior skills would fall in the areas of advanced service delivery, new approach to old problems, accelerated manufacturing speed, high quality – low reject ratio on manufacturing, or a top tier brand name. Superior resources go well beyond financial resources to physical resources (best in class property, most advanced plant and customized or specialized equipment), legal (defendable intellectual property, protected geographic territory, recognizable trade names), human (recognized industry leaders or experts in product development, top caliber sales people), organizational, informational (well developed and highly refined information systems with constant tracking of performance and goals) and relational (highly networked with top contacts in the your business' community).

These types of advanced resources and skills lead to sustainable competitive advantages that generally result in higher profits, improved ability to weather an economic storm and force other, less efficient competitors out of the market.

Protected and unique intellectual property

Protected and unique intellectual property relates to all facets of intellectual property including trademarks, trade names, software, manufacturing processes, recipes, product designs, patents, logos, tag lines, websites, sales and marketing material, marketing strategy, among others. These factors can contribute to making a company unique and to be viewed as having superior quality which translates into increased margins, an ability to withstand external pressures and overall attractiveness to purchasers, and higher valuations.

Contracted and recurring ongoing revenue streams

Recurring revenue streams are one of the keys to higher valuations. At the extreme end a utility company with little or no growth would typically have a very high valuation, because of the low risk of variability to the income stream.

Track record of continued and sustainable growth

Nothing improves the value of a business like a track record of continued and growing revenue, income and cash flow. While this cannot be impacted in one year alone, what can be done in one year is an improvement over the prior year along with the factors that have been implemented permanently over the last year that will contribute to a future sustainable growth trend.

Top level financial performance in respective industry or segment

Always compare your financial performance to your industry peers to see where your company stands, where it is performing better and the areas that can be improved upon. This is based on the simple premise that if others are performing at a higher, more profitable level, so can your business. The advantage of knowing where your business stands is that you can only fix what you know needs fixing. Otherwise you are operating blindly. Comparative financial performance can be used to assess profitability levels, liquidity ratios, debt to capital ratios and overall revenue levels. There is one key to this component and that is many company owners consider their businesses as "best in class". If this is stated to be a fact by the business owner as a way of positioning business for sale it can truly work against the value of a business if this is not the case, but if it is in fact true and can be demonstrated then the value increases dramatically based on the fact that top performing companies invariably attract premium values in the marketplace. This simple process can be done for free by visiting the library and looking for the information about your industry in the Risk Measurement Associates ("RMA") annual statement studies.

Developed, documented and systematized business processes

This is one of the key indicators or differences between a formal, professional business and a 'just a job' for the business owner. This is because the existence and documentation of systems shows that someone else is carrying out the processes and managing the operations other than the owner. Meaning that if the business owner is not there on a day-to-day basis the business can still operate, pay the owner a salary or bonus and he can be on the beach enjoying life. The documentation of systems or standard operating procedures are typically included in all areas of the business – each department and include: operational reporting, planning and scheduling productions, budgeting, best demonstrated performance and quick look reporting.

Ongoing and ingrained continual improvement program

Purchasers like to see a business where continuous improvement is built into the operational ethos. It bodes well for post-acquisition prospects.

Solid balance sheet

As discussed elsewhere in this book, the condition of your balance sheet – working capital, long-term debt etc. will feed into valuation.

Top tier management team operating independently of ownership or shareholder group

Financial purchasers will need to have a management team that can continue to operate the business post acquisition. If you already have that team in place you will save them the time, effort and business risk that goes into placing a new team with the corresponding positive effect on valuation.

No great thing is created suddenly.

- Epictetus

CHAPTER 17

Steps to Maximizing the Deal Value of Your Business

If a man is proud of his wealth, he should not be praised until it is known how he employs it.

– *Socrates*

After many years of hard work in building your business, it can be very imposing to be faced with the prospect of putting it up for sale. Rightfully you want to obtain maximum value for your hard work, however you may doubt whether you are in fact doing everything possible to obtain maximum value, if not at least fair value.

Here are some steps, some simple and some more involved, that you can take within your existing business to increase the value of your business in advance of putting it on the market.

Obtain customer contracts

Sign contracts with customers to create revenue certainty. Often customer relationships are informal based on a lifetime of working together. As such, many long-term small medium businesses do not have customer contracts, but rather have informal, non-written, agreements. While this is sufficient for your business given you (the Owner) have long-term relationships with your customers, you should recognize that the new owner will not have the benefit of your relationship(s) and in order to give you maximum value for those relationships, they will want to obtain comfort that this customer will not disappear after the sale closes. Ensuring your customer arrangements are properly documented in the form of written, ideally long-term, contracts will go a long way in providing the potential new owner the comfort they need.

Clean-up your customer list

Ensure your customer list is fully up to date, complete and integrated into a formal marketing program. Your relationship with your customers/clients is the only true asset in your business that generates income. It goes without saying, without your customers you do not have a business.

Transfer knowledge

Transfer management knowledge and responsibilities beyond ownership (you). New owners will want to know that your business can run without you or, at a minimum that steps are being taken to pass along your knowledge to key management over the course of a transition period (e.g. 2-3 year period). Hopefully you have been working on this far prior to putting your business up for sale, but in any case you need to show that you have (or are) transitioned key tasks to key managers who the purchaser will look to retain after the transaction closes. To the extent the purchaser believes the business begins and ends with you, they will be challenged to pay maximum value.

Document processes, policies and procedures

Formalize and document key systems and processes. There is a wealth of knowledge of your business that resides in both your and your employees' heads. Many businesses both small and large are so busy with day to day operations that they do not take the time to document and record internal systems, processes, etc. Documenting these processes will give purchaser's comfort that the company's success can be sustained in not only your absence, but your employees as well.

Cut personal spending

Owners will often run, to varying degrees, some personal expenses through the company. You should cut this spending out of the company as soon as possible. This will result in lower expense and higher profitability. While one might argue that these expenses can simply be added back as a normalization adjustment, as discussed in Chapter 6 you want to avoid having too many normalization adjustments and thus losing credibility.

Clean-up your books and sharpen internal accounting and reporting
It is very simple, the better and more accurate your internal
accounting and reporting capabilities the easier it will be to sell your
business. A potential purchaser will not have your familiarity and
intuitive feel for the business. They will be relying to a large degree
on their due diligence of the accounting and operational reporting
materials to help make their final decision.

Develop meaningful monthly reporting

Quick look (Dashboard) reporting - Implement quick look
reporting to actually impact the performance of your business on
a timely basis. A quick-look report is designed for the owners or
upper-management of the company, and consists of the important
measurements that give you a check on the health of your company.
The items to include in your quick-look report will be primarily
those items from your operational and financial reporting systems,
with their associated standards, that you have identified as important
to the functioning of your company. Remember that these are only
those items you need to look at in an overall management sense to
make sure that your departments are performing properly. Think
of this report as a condensed version of all your other financial and
operational reporting. It is a powerful concept that is well worth
setting up and keeping current. An owner can receive the one-page
quick-look report any morning, even on vacation by email and can
quickly be comfortable with how the company is doing or where the
company needs some attention.

Get your financial statements audited or reviewed

Your business should have accountant reviewed or audited financial
statements. If you have not done so already, you should get your
financial statements audited (best) or reviewed (better) by a reputable
accounting firm. We recommend having at least the last two years
audited or reviewed. Having your financial statements audited or
reviewed will lend creditability to the financial results and thus

give the purchaser more comfort. Having only internally prepared financial statements may be considered a "red flag" for potential purchasers. It is highly likely that without reviewed or audited financial statements, your business valuation will be discounted due to uncertainties, or perceived higher risk, in the numbers. An audit will take time and money now but save you in the end.

In addition to the above, you might also consider these additional items which while much challenging, could significantly enhance the purchase price you may be able to realize.

Focus efforts on most profitable business activities or those with most upside

Assess and rationalize your business according to profit contribution of different business activities and allocate resources to most profitable activities. Too often owners focus equal amounts of time or efforts on all aspects of their business or, worse yet, they focus more on the "troubled" activities or segments or business lines. You should prepare and execute a short-medium term business plan that is focused on.

Have employees focused on performance improvements

Consider implementing weekly workshops with key employees on ways to improve the business – corporate culture of continual process improvement.

Develop new revenue streams or product lines

While this may not be as simple as it sounds, if you considered new revenue streams or product lines, and they can be added without disrupting the steady-state business, you should consider them. You should be prepared to explain, and support, to potential buyers why these new revenue streams are sustainable into the future.

Consider acquiring a complementary business

The idea is that the value and performance of two companies combined may be greater than the sum of the separate individual companies. The potential financial benefit achieved through the combining of companies, is often a driving force behind an acquisition, and can be attributed to various factors, such as increased revenues, combined talent and technology, or cost reduction. There is of course a cost of acquiring another company and to the extent that, amongst other things, the sum of the parts is not greater than the companies on their own, an acquisition likely does not make sense for you.

While there are many things that you can do to increase the value you will receive from a purchaser, it has likely now become clear to you that the planning phase of the selling process cannot begin too early.

Invest in expansion of capacity

Always be looking to grow your business, but certainly in a prudent manner. Look to invest in the next piece of equipment to improve efficiencies or the new additional sales person that will help grow your business into a new segment or industry. These initiatives show a business and management team that are conditioned to never settle for the status quo, and always push things to the next level.

Growth initiatives

According to many marketing specialists there are only three real ways to grow a business and they represent the next items on this list. The first is to increase the number of customers you do business with. This can be done by reaching new customers 1) with your existing offering or 2) developing a new offering. Ideally you will leverage the offering you have to enter a new market or expand the reach in your existing market. Advertising that can be specifically tracked to see how many new potential customers can be attributed to each new marketing initiative. Make sure you do not spend any money on advertising that cannot be tracked for effectiveness on how much each dollar spent actually contributes to increasing your business.

Secondly, to grow your business you can increase the frequency of transactions with your customers/clients by making it as easy as possible for your clients to do business with you and to do it more and more and more. Build customer loyalty so that whenever they have to make a purchase that involves products you offer they will only go to you and not even consider your competitors. You can also do this by offering your customers new solutions that meet the needs they are getting filled elsewhere.

Lastly, you can increase transaction size with your customers. This can be done in a number of ways. Firstly increase your prices. Often the one thing true entrepreneurs know that other business owners don't or are afraid to face or find out is how truly elastic pricing really is. So many businesses are charging less than they should and much less than they could. Many more claim that their business is different but yet they actually do compete only on price. To improve sustainable value - get out of commodity businesses by doing something different so that your business is the only logical choice for your customers regardless of price.

Business maximization strategy

As has been discussed throughout the book only the best run and most profitable companies will ever actually sell. In order to ensure your company sells the implementation of business maximization strategies will contribute to the business selling and for highest price. Business maximization strategies include but are not limited to:

- Growth plans including expansion of market share as well as increased diversification of customer mix

- Sale of non-core assets or underperforming product lines or divisions

- Implementation of a formal continuous improvement program
- Reduction of operating and input costs
- Reduction of discretionary expenses
- Management training programs to increase the competence, responsibility and effectiveness of the management team (once the current owner exist the business)

One secret of success
in life is for a man
to be ready for his
opportunity when it
comes.

- Benjamin Disraeli

CHAPTER 18

Transaction
Structure
Considerations

The average long-term experience in investing is never surprising, but the short term experience is always surprising.

— *Charles Ellis*

The form of a transaction is one of the first elements of a deal to be considered, whether it is a share deal or asset deal will depend on the goals and perspectives of both the purchaser and the vendor. Typically a purchaser prefers the transaction to take the form of an asset sale due, in part, to the termination of corporate liabilities and the clean slate for the business going forward. A vendor on the other hand typically prefers a sale of shares due to preferential tax treatment.

Following the form of the transaction is transaction structure and types of consideration. These elements can have a major impact on the ultimate attractiveness or legitimacy of a deal. A business owner may come across several types of consideration in the course of negotiating the sale of a business.

Transaction structure and types of consideration can have a major impact on the ultimate attractiveness or legitimacy of a deal. A business owner may come across several types of consideration in the course of negotiating the sale of a business.

Cash – obviously a high component of cash is important in assessing the value of deal consideration. There are typically no strings attached to cash. Furthermore a component of cash will be required to pay taxes and transaction fees.

It probably goes without saying that the higher component of cash the better but there are other factors to consider including where the cash will come from to fund the deal. A common approach to fund private company transactions is to use the target company's (your company's) balance sheet to raise debt to pay for the transaction. What this means is that your company's once clean, debt free balance sheet will be fully "levered up" with all the debt you were always loathe to take on. In a simultaneous debt financing and acquisition closing - the cash for your company would come from…your company.

The best scenario is that the cash comes from a purchaser's own coffers that is fully independent of your company's resources. It is worth noting though that in almost no circumstances will transaction consideration be 100% cash, typically cash will comprise somewhere between 50% and 80% cash, with the remainder being comprised of other types of consideration, discussed below.

Vendor note, vendor loan or vendor financing. It is standard for vendor take back financing to comprise between 25% and up to 50% of a transaction. These arrangements also usually carry a low rate of interest, less than 5%. A vendor financing arrangement is in effect a derivative of the debt raised from a bank to support the transaction, it is effectively you, the business owner acting as the bank where you will be paid from your company's profits over a period of several years. The disadvantages of this type of consideration is that although it is your businesses profits funding this component of the transaction, you may not be in control of how the company performs and may be uncertain of the effectiveness of the new acquirer in running the business post transaction. This single business exposure was positive when you were at the helm of the business but may be an additional risk since you are now looking for the exit, The second drawback to this structure is that the vendor financing will be fully subordinated to any and all bank financing, meaning the bank has to get paid before you get paid. This also ties directly into the point noted above where many acquirers will fully leverage your business to pay for the transaction – meaning your vendor financing will be at the bottom of long line of creditors. The key advantage of a vendor financing arrangement is that by accepting this type of transaction consideration you get a deal completed that may not otherwise happen.

Shares in the acquisition company are often offered as a component of transaction consideration and are often framed up in such a way as to make the transaction value appear substantially higher. These shares can be a challenging component of consideration to accurately evaluate. A transaction is complicated on its own without the additional challenge of valuing another business and what the future value of its shares could be worth.

Preferred Units – This type of consideration is similar to vendor financing or shares of the acquisition company but are superior to both as they represent a priority interest in what may be a diversified fund that pays a predictable rate of return, usually superior to the return offered under a vendor note arrangement. Where Preferred Units are backed by multiple businesses generating cash flow that balances out cyclicality or seasonality. The priority return represent the first cash flow of the businesses. Preferred Units are typically offered as a way to ensure the business owner believes in their own business as a new component of the fund that will help contribute to generating cash required to pay the priority distributions and also in the fund itself as a business partner. Preferred Units also create continuity in the relationship between the business owners and the fund that acquires his company.

Earnouts or installment payments are a form of deferred or future consideration that are structured based on and tied to the future results of the business. Earnouts are often used as a way to bridge expectation gaps between the vendor (business owner) and the buyer (acquisition group). This can be a positive way for a business owner to realize additional value for a transaction.

All of these elements together can be combined to create a transaction purchase price. It is often said that the most important elements of a deal are the terms and structure rather than the price. We believe this to be the case and if you are offered a deal that represents a fair price and you can understand the terms of the consideration offered you will likely complete a transaction that you will results in a positive outcome for your years of work in building a great business.

Having a succession plan will help ensure a business transition goes as smoothly as possible.

– Equicapita

CHAPTER 19

Putting it All Together

Effort only fully releases its reward after a person refuses to quit.

— *Napoleon Hill*

Let's take this opportunity to repeat the key steps to selling your business. The essence of this section is that you should heed the warning that by approaching the sale of your business without at least a roadmap for success, a systematized approach or a mentor with the experience to guide you through the process, may result in you leaving substantial value on the table.

Step 1.   Prepare your business for sale (as previously outlined).

Step 2.   Get a sense for the value of your business, so you can assess whether an offer you receive is a fair one. That can be done through a qualified business broker, merger & acquisition advisor or Chartered Business Valuator, or your financial advisor..

Step 3.   Prepare a confidential information memorandum ("CIM") that profiles the business. A CIM is a document similar in many ways to a business plan that incorporates, among other topics – history of the business, overview of industry, customers, competitors, employees, key management, growth opportunities, historical financial statements and a financial forecast.

Step 4.   Prepare all support documents including:

- Confidentiality agreement
- Teaser document
- Financial summary
- Normalization adjustments
- Financial forecast
- Business overview
- Competitive analysis
- Industry overview

Step 5.   Develop a list of qualified purchasers. This will often be obvious to you and it may even be a little scary to put together, because you may be worried about confidentiality issues. However don't worry about that at this stage, instead compile the list of potential purchasers, which may include: competitors, suppliers, businesses that are in similar industries, private equity firms (financial buyers) that are visible in your industry and your own management team.

Step 6.   Initiate contact with potential purchaser list on a *"no-name"* basis. This is usually done direct by telephone and not by circulating an email.

Step 7.   Execute confidentiality agreements (available from your lawyer or advisor).

Step 8.   Send out the CIM to all interested parties that have executed the confidentiality agreement.

Step 9.   To the extent possible advance all negotiations and discussions with all parties along a similar path so there are more parties "at the dance" that will drive up the price.

Step 10.   Accept offers and execute a letter of intent (available from your lawyer, or advisor).

Step 11.   Facilitate purchaser due diligence.

Step 12.   Draft and complete legal agreements.

Step 13.   Close the deal.

CHAPTER 20

Case Study

Our business is about technology, yes. But it's also about operations and customer relationships.

— *Michael Dell*

The following is a case study of a fictitious business – Homer Manufacturing Corporation. Throughout this chapter we will be referring to Homer as a case study as we delve into the details of private company transactions. Our intent is that by using Homer as an example we will shed light on some of the nuances of deals and make this often-dry topic a little more engaging. Throughout this chapter we will also be reinforcing previous topics with the idea being that this chapter could be read on its own and the key points can still be captured.

Homer has been in business since 1978. The company was started by Arthur Holmes who was at the time working for a large national company where he became increasingly frustrated with the progress of his career and the actions and philosophies of the company's management. So Arthur launched his small business by renting a small facility and taking along his friend in the shop who was a master of *"making things work."* Arthur is a good salesman so he brought in the business and his first employee looked after filling the orders.

The company was financed principally with Arthur's life savings and after several years of struggle for him and his family, Arthur carved out a small niche in the widget sector by delivering reliable products on time and with a focus on delivering better customer service than his competitors.

Over the years the business outgrew the rented facility, though not steadily, and Arthur purchased a parcel of land and an industrial building with 20,000 square feet of manufacturing space. The company continued to grow, expand its product offering and increase its customer base. In 1996 the company purchased a new facility to increase overall capacity.

Over time Arthur maintained a solid relationship with the bank and was able to secure both term financing for acquisition of expansion capital expenditures and an operating line of credit to provide the necessary liquidity in times of ups and downs. Arthur's children have become successful in their own right with his son Arthur Jr. becoming a doctor and his daughter Jane, a lawyer – neither of them was interested in taking over the business.

The company as it stands now has 70 employees, including a professional management team that look after the managing the operations and weighs in on strategic decisions in conjunction with Arthur. A solid operational management team, reporting to executive management, looks after the day-to-day operations. Revenue is approximately $25,000,000 with EBITDA of $2,000,000. The business also has an authorized operating line of credit with Bank of Western Canada for $2.5 million, of which it typically only draws on the line as seasonal working capital requirements increase. In addition, Arthur is a meticulous businessman who over time has put together detailed operating manuals and written processes for his business. Arthur also cares a great deal about his employees as they are like members of the family and so the company has implemented an award winning safety program with a certificate of recognition from the province.

Arthur Holmes is now 64 years old and has decided that although he has passed most of the day to day responsibilities to his management team he would like to "cash out" after over 30 years of his life invested in growing, struggling and managing this business. He is contemplating several different options including a sale to a competitor or industry insider, a sale to his management team (though he still wants to maximize his proceeds) and a sale to a financial investor or private equity group.

Homer's strong management team is led by Bob Portman age 46. Bob is the general manager who looks after all the operations, has been with the company for 10 years and has for the most part spent his career in the industry. Bob's leadership skills have shown in his ability to attract some of the best people in the industry to

Homer and keep them over the long term, in part, by simply being great with people, and a real teacher and investor in people's career development. Bob has demonstrated the type of initiative that would be characterized as entrepreneurial spirit but he has always operated with that philosophy as an employee instead of taking the risks an entrepreneur does.

In addition, there is a strong financial manager, Cathy Fernandez, who although her title is finance and accounting manager, she really acts as the Chief Financial Officer as she is responsible for dealing with the banks, arranging lease and other financing and prepares reports for the management committee. Cathy, 39, has been with the business for 12 years.

The third key member of the management team is Paul Schimkowski, who is the sales manager. Paul, 50, would not be classified as your stereotypical salesman as he is actually fairly quiet, but very knowledgeable about the business and about what his clients really want. Paul has been with the business for over 20 years. Recently he proved his value by saving the loss of the largest customer through solid customer attentiveness and shrewd negotiating.

Cathy Fernandez has a very good handle on the financial picture of the business and is often explaining the details of the financial picture to Bob and Paul.

These three managers work well together but occasionally have their differences though they do have one thing in common – a belief in the long-term success of Homer. The trio had approached Arthur about orchestrating a management buyout as one of his options to get his money out of the business but felt perhaps it was beyond their means. Regardless, Arthur has been open and kept them informed about his retirement plans and in return they are keen to assist in the sale and to transition their involvement to a new owner.

Some of this section will also be in the form of dialogue between Arthur, Cathy, Paul and Bob and other characters as they become relevant to the situation.

Homer would be considered a top-quartile performer in its industry segment. When highlighting how the different situations and characteristics of deals are encountered we will refer to Homer and often compare the impact on a deal of a top performer to average performers or lower quartile companies to demonstrate the differences.

Homer's business is described as fabricated metal products manufacturing with an SIC code of 3499. The following is a snapshot of the balance sheet and income statement of Homer:

Income Statement	
Sales	$25,000,000
Cost of Sales	$16,625,000
Gross Profit	$8,375,000
Operating Expenses	$4,750,000
Operating Profit	$3,625,000
Other Expenses	$2,077,000
Profit Before Taxes	$1,548,000
Interest on Long term debt	$187,000
Depreciation & amortization	$265,000
EBITDA	$2,000,000

Balance Sheet	
Assets	
Cash & Equivalents	$541,645
Trade Receivables (net)	$3,125,000
Inventory	$1,354,010
All Other Current Assets	$391,651
Total Current Assets	$5,412,306
Fixed Assets (net)	$2,212,389
Intangible Assets	$341,653
All Other Non-Current Assets	$366,652
Total	$8,333,000
Liabilities	
Trade Payables	$865,885
Notes Payable - Short Term	$941,629
Current Maturity L/T/D	$259,579
Income Taxes Payable	$16,666
All Other Current Liabilities	$858,299
Total Current Liabilities	$2,942,058
Long-Term Debt	$1,297,893
Deferred Taxes	$49,998
All Other Non-Current Debt	$516,646
Total	$4,806,595
Equity	
Equity	$3,526,405
Total Liabilities & Equity	$8,333,000

Why most businesses never sell?

Arthur returned from a Rotary lunch meeting where they had a guest speaker talking about selling businesses where the topic of the speech was "why most businesses never sell – and what you can do about it". The talk for this group was on target as many of the members of Arthur's rotary club are business owners and several are considering selling their businesses as they are at or near conventionally viewed "retirement age" Arthur talked to Cathy about this lunch as was somewhat troubled by the topic given what he is planning for Homer.

Statistics suggest that when customers complain, business owners and managers ought to get excited about it. The complaining customer represents a huge opportunity for more business.

— *Zig Ziglar*

"Cathy did you know that at any given time as many as 10% of all businesses are "for sale" and of those businesses only 25% actually ever sell?"

"No Arthur, I wasn't aware of that – but I don't think you have to worry about that you have a solid business that many groups would love to own"

"Well that may be Cathy, but this speaker today explained that there are three common mistakes that business owners often make when they go to sell their businesses. They typically have no idea what the business is really worth and as such when they receive an offer they are either insulted that it is lower than they think it should be worth, they expect more than it is actually worth and as such can never get a deal done based purely on stubbornness because no one can see the "true" value and lastly they go about the sales process in entirely the wrong way.

Cathy replied "This may appear self-serving but don't forget about the fact that Bob, Paul and I would like to be considered as the next owners"

"I appreciate that Cathy, but to be frank we are talking about my life's work – I want to get fair value for it.

Cathy nodded.

Arthur recalled to himself that this gentlemen explained that the businesses are often inappropriately positioned with prospective purchasers, management is not kept in mind as to the future plans for the business and they sometimes leave the business so he added *"Cathy I do want to assure you though whatever the outcome you, Bob and Paul will be integral to the ongoing business, either as owners or key executives"* and followed with *"I feel like this process will be similar to selling a house – we have to make the business easy to buy and looking its best. I want to make sure that whoever buys this business sees it as a great business, at a fair price and as a great package and platform for continued profitability and growth and that includes you guys as the management team if you are the successful buyer."*

Preparing Homer For Sale

What can be done in advance of selling to increase the value of your business?

A few days later Arthur called his second in command, Bob Portman, into his office *"Hey Bob,"* Arthur said to *"I just got back from a meeting with my accountant and he had an investment banker sit in on the meeting and this guy really seemed to know what he was talking about."*

"He said that the planning component of the selling process of your business cannot begin too early – I am worried we may have waited too long if I expect to sell to you guys or another group in 6 months."

"Fortunately he did say that there were several factors that contribute to the "saleability" and attractiveness of any business that we could work on right away"

Bob smiled as he had been saying to Arthur for years that a business is like a house in order to make it easy to sell you have to get it ready so the sale process will become that much smoother.

The overriding message is that for a business that took many years, even decades to build for which a value of many millions of dollars is locked up it is worth any effort necessary to go through some simple, though not necessarily easy steps to increasing that overall value, likelihood of sale and actual amount of cash received when the business is sold.

If you assume the value of a business is $10 million today, by working through the following key areas over the period of a year the value could be increased substantially and the business could sell in a much shorter period of time than it would take if the business is not finely tuned and ready for sale.

> *"Guys I called you together today to give you an update on where things stand on the sale of the business"* Arthur said to his management team – Bob, Cathy and Paul *"This is a stressful process and I appreciate all that you guys have been doing along the way – the plan we put together is going to make all the difference"*.

Selling your business could truly be one of the most stressful and emotional experiences of your business life. To make the process run smoothly there are several factors that can be addressed in advance of a transaction. The considerations outlined below will provide insight into the best ways to prepare your business for sale and maximize the value once you sell.

Always have in the back of your mind that it is estimated that half of Canadian small-business owners plan to retire and transfer control of their business by 2019[11] while typically only 10% of all independent business owners have a formal plan to sell or transfer their business. A sale plan is critical and given how few businesses have one it can be a critical advantage during the process.

> Arthur walked into Bob's office *"Bob, the more I speak to my business owner friends, the more I see that we are all considering selling and retirement. That's new to me, it seems like just a few years ago our only concerns were growing the business - getting new customers, keeping old*

Profit in business comes from repeat customers, customers that boast about your project or service, and that bring friends with them.

– W. Edwards Deming

ones happy. If everyone is looking to do the same thing at the same time, I need an edge to ensure that my sale goes smoothly. I want us to put together a plan including some thoughts on succession. You guys are a part of this process and I want to make sure you are up to speed."

Having a succession plan will help ensure a business transition goes as smoothly as possible. A well-designed succession plan will help ensure the future financial stability and value of the business.

A plan will also encourage you to focus on the tax issues surrounding a sale and hopefully reduce the potential tax liabilities of transferring the ownership. You want to set a timetable for transfer of ownership to the successor, whether a family member, employee or an outside purchaser and start to work to that schedule. An organized plan also helps you manage your time so that while the sales process in underway you and key managers can continue to contribute to the growth of the business in terms of market share, profitability and size, and knowing what the future holds will provide stability for employees.

The downside of not planning is undeniable: unprepared owners will be forced to sell at a discount with the associated risk of business closure and loss of jobs.[12]

Once the decision has been made to sell a business, it can take up to one year to prepare the business to receive the highest price, one year until the deal is completed and a further six months to fully exit from day to day operations. If you are considering selling your business with the plan of being out in three years or less, the best time to start the process is today.

Arthur meets Bob in the hallway and starts to chat about the future *"Bob you and your wife Sally bought a place out on Lake Pleasant didn't you? You know me and Angela were thinking about where we might like to buy a country place to spend some time on and off now and then far more in retirement. When I think of what we have to do to conclude a sale, I realize that it will be years before anything is final."*

Bob replied *"Arthur, me and the rest of the management team love working here and are as keen as you to get a sale done to the right buyer at the right price. We are glad you have included us in your planning and I know that over the course of the next couple of years we can get this done right – both for you and for us because it's like family here and we look out for each other."*

Bob then added *"Under your leadership we have built a great business – we have all the policies, procedures and processes documented and ingrained in the culture. The business always looks good – as we are always prepared to give a tour when potential customers drop in and most importantly we know we are a top performer compared to our peers – you will have no problem selling your business."*

A transfer of your business to the next generation is not generally the best solution for the sustainability of the business. Only 33% of family businesses survive from the first generation into the second while only 15% survive into the third generation.[13]

Selling your business has some parallels to selling your house...you must ensure that your business "shows well". Make sure the office and shop are clean and organized, a disorganized or messy business is a "red-flag" to investors as it raises the concerns there could be "messes" elsewhere in the business, like the financial statements.

Make the business easy to buy... Have in place detailed operating manuals and procedures as well as a second tier of management that will make the transition for new owners a smooth one. The last thing you want is for a potential purchaser to believe that once you are gone, so will the business.

Now we would like to turn your attention to how a succession plan can enhance value.

> *"You know Bob"* Cathy said over lunch *"Arthur is constantly talking about who might buy the business. We know he doesn't have a succession plan because if he did I think he might actually get more for his business than just simply reacting to whatever comes his way."*

A succession plan is one of the foundational elements of a company with a long-term vision; even Fortune 500 companies must have succession plans in place to ensure their longevity. Of course a succession plan for a private company will likely differ from that of a Fortune 500 company but many of the same elements will be present in both.

Distribution of ownership or exit strategy

This will relate to whether or not the succession plan is one where ownership will remain in the family or with the current shareholder group and their family or whether the succession will include a sale to a third party – be it a strategic purchaser, a financial purchaser or the management team. This is essentially an either or decision – will the current ownership retain ownership after their management services are severed or will they sell the business.

> Arthur asked Cathy one day *"Do you think a buyer is going to want me around after a sale? I'm not sure if I want to stay as a minority shareholder, just a consultant or exit the business completely leaving you guys in charge for the new owner."* Cathy replied *"That is really going to depend on the buyer, best for you to have a clear idea of outcome you want*

and then work to find the buyer who can accommodate you. Remember that a smooth management transition is what all buyers are looking for. If you can show that is possible it is much easier to structure the deal you want."

Who will take over leading the business?

Whether you plan to keep the ownership internal or move it external, the president/CEO cannot remain at the helm forever and a new one must be chosen, searched for or groomed. Someone has to lead the business in order for it maintain and grow the value, and for it to execute on its short and long term goals and objectives.

Critical factors to consider when the time comes to sell your business.

"Well team I think we are ready to sell the business, after almost one year of making all the changes as recommended to us as well as implementing some new initiatives not only is the business worth more but it is also ready to sell" Arthur said to Paul, Bob and Cathy. *"Now I won't forget all the hard work you guys have contributed to this process and I will give you guys a fair chance to buy the business – after all I owe a lot to you."*

Mechanics of the Sale

This includes the details of the three major scenarios.

- Outright sale - How much would you be willing to provide as financing (vendor note, second mortgage on real estate) and would you be willing to take consideration other than cash as a way to increase the overall proceeds (earnout, shares in the purchase company) What is being sold? – The shares, the operating assets, everything including company owned real estate.

- Management buyout - Same as above including do you want to sell 100% of the company or do you want to retain a component of the business to facilitate the purchase.

- Transition to family members - How will you ensure you get some cash out of your business? What type of financial assistance you will provide to facilitate the transaction and provide comfort to the financial institutions that the business will succeed once you have exited the business.

Timeline. A clear plan should be in place that includes a detailed timeline so that that the people involved know what to expect and what will be involved in the program. To the extent possible fuzzy generalities should be avoided since there will be nothing to stick to when the process begins.

Contingency considerations and progress monitoring. To paraphrase Robert Burns - the best-laid plans often go awry. Therefore, it is important to:

- Contingency plan – if the key shareholder or owner becomes suddenly sick or dies, the business may be in jeopardy due to the delay in transitioning key relationships, responsibilities or other roles. One of the best ways to deal with these contingencies is key man insurance that would fund the business in case of such a loss. The second way is to not delay in grooming your successor.

- Monitor the progress of the plan along the way to see if things are moving along as planned, as well if things do get off track how to get them back on track.

"Paul what do you think of this idea that we have to prepare Homer for sale by working on selling the sizzle? This is a great business anyone can see that. I don't like the sound of trying to make up things - do you?"

I have always said that everyone is in sales. Maybe you don't hold the title of salesperson, but if the business you are in requires you to deal with people, you, my friend, are in sales.

– Zig Ziglar

"Well Arthur in my experience in sales even the greatest product has to be positioned with the customer – you have to make sure they understand what they are getting when they buy and how the product addresses their needs. I don't think that selling Homer is any different really."

As we have emphasized several times before in this book, you will only sell your business once and therefore you will want to ensure that the transaction goes as smoothly as possible and that you achieve the highest price for your business. The critical factors outlined below will provide insight into the best ways to ensure your business sells and you receive the maximum value.

If you decide to sell your business and it is inadequately marketed, inappropriately represented or improperly valued the business will likely not sell. With have mentioned this statistic several times before but it is always worth repeating. As many as 15% of private businesses are for sale at any one time and of those for sale, only 25% of those are ever sold. The others are either shut down, the assets are simply liquidated or the business owner continues to be involved. How the business is positioned and marketed can be as important to the ultimate sale outcome as the quality of the business itself. Ensure the firm you choose to represent you for your sale transaction has a proven system.

The business sale process can go on forever. Without a systematized, proactive process a business can be perpetually on the market. If you work with a firm with a proven system for getting results your ultimate success is greatly improved.

A major issue faced by successors (purchasers of the business) is the financing of the business acquisition. When selling your business ensure that you are represented by sophisticated advisors who are familiar with structuring business acquisition financing so that they can provide guidance to both you and the purchaser in ensuring the deal will be successfully completed.

When you decide to sell your business ensure you are not at a disadvantage when you are negotiating with a seasoned business acquirer. Since you have one opportunity to sell your business and you may sell your business to a purchaser that has completed many transactions you will want to ensure that you have an advisor or mentor on your side that is expert in negotiating and structuring sale transactions.

Deal with an advisor that will give you the time and attention your business deserves. Should you decide that you are going to hire a professional advisor to sell your business ensure that the advisor you select will dedicate their time to your project and that most of the work will not be downloaded on to a junior team member.

Key steps to selling your business. There are typical processes involved in selling any business and it is important to keep these steps in mind when you go to sell your business. While you may save money by selling your business without a broker, you should heed the warning that by approaching the sale of your business without at least a roadmap for success, a systematized approach or a Mentor with the experience to guide you through the process you may sell your business but you may leave a load of money on the table.

Step 1.   Prepare your business for sale (as outlined in elsewhere in this book). This is often best accomplished by hiring a professional corporate finance/Mergers & Acquisitions firm to manage the complex process for you.

Step 2.   Get a sense for the value of your business so you can assess whether an offer you receive is a fair one. That can be done through a qualified business valuator or through a mentoring program that provides that service at the outset of the program.

Business valuation. How do you know what a good price is for your business until you get an objective and definitive perspective on what the actual value of the business? This is an important and necessary first step of the succession plan. This coupled with the business maximization strategy will determine the baseline value for the business and programs to put in place to increase the overall value of the business.

Step 3. Prepare a Confidential Information Memorandum or Business Plan that profiles the business.

Step 4. Prepare all support documents including:

- Confidentiality agreement
- Teaser document
- Financial summary
- Normalization adjustments
- Financial forecast
- Business overview
- Competitive analysis
- Industry overview

Step 5. Develop your list of potentially qualified purchasers. This will often be obvious to you and it may even be a little scary to put together because you may be worried about confidentiality issues. But don't worry about that at this stage, instead compile the list with all the potential purchasers that may include but is probably not limited to competitors, suppliers, businesses that are in similar industries, private equity firms (financial

An organization, no matter how well designed, is only as good as the people who live and work in it.

– *Dee Hock*

buyers) that are visible in your industry, your own management team.

Step 6. Initiate contact with purchaser list on a "no-names" basis. This is usually done direct by telephone and not by merely sending an email to a list.

Step 7. Execute confidentiality agreements (available from your lawyer, advisor or mentoring program).

Step 8. Send out the CIM to all interested parties that have executed the confidentiality agreement.

Step 9. To the extent possible advance all negotiations and discussions with all parties along a similar path so there are more parties *"at the dance"* that will drive up the price.

Step 10. Accept offers and execute letter of intent (available from your lawyer, advisor or mentoring program).

Step 11. Facilitate purchaser due diligence.

Step 12. Draft and complete legal agreements.

Step 13. Close the deal and cash the cheque.

Factors Impacting Value

The following are a non-exhaustive series of factors that we believe contribute to higher business values.

Arthur opened the executive meeting with a reminder of the upcoming strategy retreat *"Team I want to remind you that we are going to be out of the office for the next two days formulating our 5 year plan. We are doing this so that even if we are not able to sell the business we will be able to continue to monitor our success. I expect you guys to be ready to be engaged in the process – after all it may be your business eventually!"*

Develop a vision for the business that corresponds to a five year business plan and financial forecast. These items can be used to assess the progress of the business and as a framework for running the business and achieving the goals of the organization.

As Cathy was giving her financial update during the executive meeting she explained the current accounts receivable position "Guys we are starting to see some additional aging of accounts receivable - some of our customers are getting to be a little slower payers, we are either being too easy on them and they are using us as their bank or we have some customers that are starting to encounter some tough times – let's stay on top of it and keep our eyes and ears open for signs of trouble. We don't want to be left sitting on a bunch of bad debts."

Be disciplined in working your accounts receivable collections. Especially in tight economic times being vigilant with credit can ensure your long-term health and from a purchaser perspective it shows the business is well managed with very few bad debts or risky accounts.

Clean up all non-necessary expenses and ensure all non-business related expenses are cleared from the business. This is to show the business is run as a business not as a personal bank account for the owner.

"Also Cathy I keep hearing about "EBITDA", what happened to good, old-fashioned Net Income?" Arthur asked.

"Arthur" Cathy replied *"as you know everything is a shortcut these days. There is absolutely nothing wrong with Net Income, in fact that is what I focus on for the measurement*

of our business success along with discretionary cash flow, but EBITDA is being used and referred to more and more, just because it is easily used to compare somewhat similar, but not identical businesses"

"Cathy do we really need to go to all the time and cost of getting audited financial statements? We have been using our internal financials since I started this business and they always have been good enough."

"Well Arthur I believe it actually can be done quite quickly, we already have a lot of the information in our accounting system. The cost for a business our size should be reasonable and I understand that we stand a good chance of recovering of more than recovering that money by getting a better sale price."

Your business should have accountant reviewed or audited financial statements. Internally prepared financial statements are considered a "red flag" for purchasers because there is potential or perception for manipulation of financial results. Consider audited or reviewed financial statements an investment in your business.

Solid balance sheet. As little debt as possible and if you have it make sure it is on the best and most flexible terms such that a purchaser would consider assuming the debt as opposed to arranging their own.

Understand how your business's performance compares to other businesses in the same or similar industries. Buyers often hear the claims "my business is a best in class performer" or "we are a top-quartile company" and they usually are skeptical. Ensure that before you present your business for sale that you do in fact know how your business stacks up from both a profitability and balance sheet perspective versus other companies in your industry because astute businesses purchasers will certainly have that information.

Top level financial performance in respective industry or segment. Always compare your financial performance to your industry peers to see where your company stands, where it is performing better and the areas that can be improved upon. This is based on the simple premise that if others are performing at a higher, more profitable level, so can your business. The advantage of knowing where your business stands is that you can only fix what you know needs fixing. Otherwise you are operating blindly. Comparative financial performance can be used to assess profitability levels, liquidity ratios, debt to capital ratios, and overall revenue levels. There is one key to this component and that is many company owners consider their businesses as "best in class".

If this is stated to be a fact by the business owner as a way of positioning business for sale it can truly work against the value of a business if this is not the case but if it is in fact true and can be definitively demonstrated then the value increases dramatically based on the fact that top performing companies always garner premium values in the marketplace. This simple process can be done for free by visiting the library and looking for the information about your industry in the RMA annual statement studies.

> At the conclusion of the executive meeting Cathy caught Arthur before he left for his two weeks holidays *"Arthur don't forget if you get antsy while you are on the golf course – don't forget you can pull up your quick report on your iphone – you will be able to see our new orders, updated backlog, number of items shipped and cash collected among other things – this report should put your mind at ease so you can enjoy your holiday!"*

High quality financial records

Not simply year end financials but actual timely operational reporting that the management team can use as a resource to determine what may need fixing and give them the opportunity to fix it quickly. We refer to this as quick look reporting or even "owner on the beach" reporting – This report should include the ten key drivers or factors in your business that can be reported on each day that you can have a quick look at to see how the business is doing and by glancing you can see how the results will be next month or 60 days out. Some examples of these items can include backlog, daily production, daily sales, last week's sales, new orders received, cash collected today or over the last week, new customer inquiries, etc.

Use quick look reporting to actually impact your business on a timely basis

Implement quick look reporting to actually impact the performance of your business on a timely basis. A quick-look report is designed for the owners or upper-management of the company, and consists of the important measurements that give you a check on the health of your company. The items to include in your quick-look report will be primarily those items from your operational and financial reporting systems, with their associated standards, that you have identified as important to the functioning of your company. Remember that these are only those items you need to look at in an overall management sense to make sure that your departments are performing properly. Think of this report as a condensed version of all your other financial and operational reporting. It is a powerful concept that is well worth setting up and keeping current. An owner can receive the one-page quick-look report any morning, even on vacation by email or by a dedicated website, and can quickly be comfortable with how the company is doing or where the company needs some attention.

Ability to integrate acquisitions into the main company or scalability to expand the operations

Be a platform company that can demonstrate the ability to buy a company, integrate it and make more profit than there was previously in the two separate companies. This really shows that a management

You do not get what you want. You get what you negotiate.

— *Harvey Mackay*

team knows what they are doing and represents a huge incremental value to a potential purchaser.

Assess and rationalize your business according to profit contribution – and be ruthless about it

When a business unit or product line is not contributing its fair share of profit or return on capital employed in that part of the business then it should be closed down or terminated. That product line or business unit is probably draining more than cash from the rest of the business it is probably draining your employees' valuable time that could be spent in more profitable areas of the business or even exploring new solutions to offer to you client base.

Invest in expansion of capacity

Always be looking to grow your business, but certainly in a prudent manner. Look to invest in the next piece of equipment to improve efficiencies or the new additional sales person that will help grow your business into a new segment or industry. These initiatives show a business and management team that are conditioned to never settle for the status quo, and always push things to the next level.

Well documented business processes

This is one of the key indicators or differences between a formal, professional business and a just a job for the business owner. This is because the existence and documentation of systems shows that someone else is carrying out the processes and managing the operations other than the owner. Meaning that if the business owner is not there on a day-to-day basis the business can still operate, pay the owner a salary or bonus and he can be on the beach enjoying life.

The documentation of systems or standard operating procedures is typically included in all areas of the business – each department and includes:

- Operational reporting
- Planning and scheduling production
- Budgeting
- Best demonstrated performance
- Quick look reporting
- Ongoing and ingrained continual improvement program

Top tier management team operating independently of the ownership or shareholder group. Transfer management responsibilities beyond the ownership group to ensure a potential purchaser sees this as a business not a job for the owner. Whether the purchaser is a financial purchaser or strategic purchaser the better equipped your management team is to operate the business in your absence the more valuable your business is.

Role of key employees. Key employees are crucial to the health and longevity of any business and it is important to include them as part of the overall succession strategy. Furthermore by including the employees as part of the process not only will you probably get better buy-in but your will likely eliminate the spread of rumors of what will happen with the business and the uncertainty related to their jobs. As a way of mitigating the risk to the business of losing a key employee through the speculation and uncertainty of a transaction, it is best to keep key people in the loop on what is going on and what the overall plan. A further way to protect the business is obtain key man life insurance on key employees in case you lose a key employee to death at an untimely point in the business cycle.

Implement Regular Key Employee Workshops. You may be surprised how well your employees know your business and how many great ideas they have for making the business better. If you have bi-weekly employee workshops focusing on things like "How to improve customer interactions", "New ways to get referrals" and "New product improvements that would meet our customers' needs better" to name a few. This type of program encourages employee teamwork and cohesiveness as well as it gets the employees singing off the same song-sheet.

Paul Schimkowski, the sales manager has been working on some business expansion strategies and he explained in the recent manager meeting *"In order for us to increase our business we need to do two things as far as I can see it – we need new customers and we need to get more of the purchases that our customers make – we are getting squeezed on pricing a lot lately so we don't have an opportunity to really grow revenue through price increases."*

According to many marketing specialists there are only three real ways to grow a business and they represent the next items on this list. The first is to increase the number of customers you do business with. This can be done by reaching new customers 1) with your existing offering or 2) developing a new offering. Ideally you will leverage the offering you have to enter a new market or expand the reach in your existing market. Advertising that can be specifically tracked to see how many new potential customers can be attributed to each new marketing initiative. Make sure you do not spend any money on advertising that cannot be tracked for effectiveness on how much each dollar spent actually contributes to increasing your business.

Secondly, to grow your business you can increase the frequency of transactions with your customers/clients by making it as easy as possible for your clients to do business with you and to do it more and more and more. Build customer loyalty so that whenever they have to make a purchase that involves products you offer they will only go to you and not even consider your competitors. You can also do this by offering your customers new solutions that meet the needs they are getting filled elsewhere.

Lastly, you can increase transaction size with your customers. This can be done in a number of ways. Firstly increase your prices. Often the one thing true entrepreneurs know that other business owners don't or are afraid to face or find out is how truly elastic pricing really is. So many businesses are charging less than they should and much less than they could. Many more claim that their business is different but yet they actually do compete only on price. To improve sustainable value - get out of commodity businesses by doing something different so that your business is the only logical choice for your customers regardless of price.

> Bob, the strategic thinker of the group replied during the meeting *"Paul you are talking about new customers all the time, if you ask me the real value of our business lies in the value of the relationships we have with our existing customers".*

Consider total or lifetime customer value. A customer is worth more to your business than simply the first sale that is made. Consider that a new customer, if treated properly will continue to make purchases from you for many years to come. Then the value of that customer is the present value of the profit for all the years of business they do with you less the cost to acquire and maintain that customer. If you think of customers for their long-term value as opposed to single transaction value only you will be able to spend more acquiring and keeping new customers than your competitors.

Following on the lifetime value of a customer is your customer list. This is one of your most valuable assets – make it as complete, informative and up to date as humanly possible. In order to ensure you have maximum customer list value – keep in touch with your customers. Send them monthly newsletters that include announcements about your business, new initiatives, the latest product developments or introductions that would meet their needs as well as upcoming sales or promotions. The more you keep in contact with your customers and form a relationship the more valuable they become.

"While we love Arthur we know he sometimes is not big on change and new initiatives so once we take over the business and there are some things I would like us to consider" Cathy said to Bob and Paul *"we should consider laying the groundwork for some simple improvements and processes that will increase the value of the business. I have done a fair bit of research and I think these would have the most impact in the shortest possible time."*

"Good point Cathy" Paul replied *"In addition to process improvements, my work with our customers has shown that we have to continue to evolve our product offering so that we have a competitive advantage beyond price competitiveness. I think that there are real opportunities to continue to strengthen our relationship with our customers so that our competitors will be blocked at the door."*

Sustainable competitive advantage. What this really means is that if a business is in a competitive industry, where in truth every industry is competitive, it represents some type of competitive obstacle that is defendable – similar to a moat around a castle. There is no way to attack a castle without crossing the moat – well the same can be said for a sustainable competitive advantage. Typically sustainable competitive advantages result from superior skills and superior resources,[14] and cannot be readily copied by competitors.

Superior skills would fall into the areas of advanced service delivery, new approach to old problems, accelerated manufacturing speed, high quality – low reject ratio on manufacturing, top tier brand name. Superior resources go well beyond financial resources to physical resources (best in class property, most advanced plant and customized or specialized equipment), legal (defendable intellectual property, protected geographic territory, recognizable trade names), human (recognized industry leaders or experts in product development, top caliber sales people), organizational informational (well developed and highly refined information systems with constant tracking of performance and goals) and relational (highly networked with top contacts in the your business' influential community).

These types of advanced resources and skills lead to sustainable competitive advantages that generally result in higher profits over a period of time, an ability to weather a economic storm due to being the low cost producer and force out other players of the market in a price war, growing market share attributable to higher perceived quality of products or services delivered, larger and more frequent transactions with customers due to higher refined and implemented sales and marketing programs.

Protected and unique intellectual property. Protected and unique intellectual property relates to all facets of intellectual property including trademarks, trade names, software, manufacturing processes, recipes, product designs, patents, logos, tag lines, websites, sales and marketing material, marketing strategy, among others. These factors can contribute to making a company unique and to be viewed as having superior quality which translates into increased margins, an ability to withstand external pressures and overall attractiveness to purchasers, and higher valuations.

Contracted and recurring ongoing revenue streams. Recurring revenue streams are one of the keys to higher valuations. At the extreme end a utility company even with little or no growth would typically have a very high valuation, because of the low risk of variability to the income stream.

Ongoing research and development into new products or new ways of delivering service – staying ahead of the curve.

Business maximization strategy. As has been discussed throughout the book only the best run and most profitable companies will ever actually sell. In order to ensure your company sells the implementation of business maximization strategies will contribute to the business selling and for highest price. Business maximization strategies include but are not limited to:

- Growth plans including expansion of market share as well as increased diversification of customer mix

- Sale of non-core assets or underperforming product lines or divisions

- Implementation of a formal continuous improvement program

- Reduction of operating and input costs

- Reduction of discretionary expenses

- Management training programs to increase the competence, responsibility and effectiveness of the management team (once the current owner exits the business)

As Arthur was reflecting on all the dialogue and conversations he had had with his management team and with his team of advisors there was one overriding thought that kept coming back to him "We have built a great business – we have shown strong, steady growth over the last ten years that has built on the rapid early success of the business. We have demonstrated our ability to generate consistent, predictable revenue from our customers and we have put together all the pieces so that the business will run smoothly whether I am here or not."

Track record of continued and sustainable growth. Nothing improves the value of a business like a track record of continued and growing revenue, income and cash flow. While this cannot be impacted in one year alone, what can be done in one year is an improvement over the prior year along with the factors that have been implemented permanently over the last year that will contribute to a future sustainable growth trend.

The keystone of successful business is cooperation. Friction retards progress.

–*James Cash Penney*

CHAPTER 21

Why We Wrote This Book

A business absolutely devoted to service will have only one worry about profits. They will be embarrassingly large.

–Henry Ford

We wrote this book because we do not view the process of partnering with our portfolio companies as adversarial. We believe the better informed both parties at the table are, the better the outcome. In the spirit of openness we in fact encourage all potential vendors to speak to any of our existing portfolio companies – management and vendors – to learn how Equicapita differs from traditional private equity firms.

And we are definitely different - we view ourselves as custodians of the great business you have built, not someone who is coming in to save the day, generate massive growth, restructure systems that took you years to build and nurture.

Contact us any time to chat. Whether you are contemplating a sale today or in the future we want to hear from you.

No great thing is created suddenly.

– *Epictetus*

There are two ways to be fooled. One is to believe what isn't true; the other is to refuse to believe what is true.

- *Søren Kierkegaard*

Epilogue

Hopefully we achieved our purpose in this book that was to provide some guidance of best practices and background into what acquirers will look for in your business. At this point you should be more comfortable with how a purchaser might value your business and the steps you might take to maximize that value.

You have spent what may actually be or seem like a lifetime building a vibrant operation and reaching a decision to part with it may be very difficult. The key is to be objective and informed. Forearmed with the information in this book you are likely to generate a sales price that most accurately reflects the intrinsic value of your business and save valuable time and energy in the process.

If you are an owner considering selling your business please feel free to contact Equicapita to discuss your options. The "About Equicapita" section of this book contains a detailed explanation of who we are and our deal review and processing approach.

They succeed, because they think they can.

– Virgil

Luck is a dividend of sweat. The more you sweat, the luckier you get.

– *Ray Kroc*

About Equicapita and the Equicapita Deal Process

Equicapita is a Calgary based investment fund that acquires private, small and medium sized enterprises in Western Canada.

Our focus on western Canadian businesses simply comes down to macroeconomics - Western Canada has consistently generated higher rates of GDP growth than overall Canadian averages and while no region of the world is immune from growth volatility we expect higher than average western Canadian growth rates to continue for the foreseeable future. The long-term fundamentals in Western Canada are strong, underpinned by a highly entrepreneurial economy and a wide range of commodities – agriculture, potash, metals and energy.

As Alberta based entrepreneurs ourselves, we recognize the need for organized capital to partner with business owners to provide a much needed liquidity option to transition business ownership. We believe Equicapita is the solution. Our aim is continue the legacy of your business, by partnering with strong, existing management teams over a long-term investment horizon.

Equicapita is focused on acquiring a diversified portfolio of private businesses, primarily from retiring owners seeking liquidity. We seek to make majority interest equity investments, but have flexibility to collaborate with the needs of the individual business owner in structuring a suitable transaction to meet their needs. Our preferred investment criteria include:

- Long-term operating history with sustainable cash flow
- EBITDA of $1 to $5 million
- Operating margins > 10%, in stable or growing industry
- Durable competitive advantage, with consistent sales and cash flow growth
- Low to modest capital intensity
- Strong customer relationships
- Incumbent management will accept performance-linked compensation
- Ability to buy up to 100% of equity

Our preferred management situation is an:

- Owner ready to retire seeking liquidity
- Owner who wants a reduced or more focused role (e.g. business development, product development, sales)
- Divestiture from a larger corporation

In general, we are seeking companies with the following characteristics:

- Western Canadian based and focused (preferred)
- Diverse customer base, with low accounts receivable concentration
- Well positioned in growing or fragmented industry
- Strong corporate culture, with history of employee retention

Equicapita is focused on the small and medium sized private business market and does not operate like the typical private equity fund. Equicapita:

- offers a streamlined sales process;
- has the ability to move quickly and confidentially to achieve desired outcome;
- is a long-term investor, your business legacy will continue; and
- values your current employees as they are a critical piece of our forward growth strategy.

Equicapita will provide, where necessary, strategic, business, financial, accounting, and legal expertise to each business's management team but give them the autonomy to continue to operate the business.

Success is getting what you want. Happiness is wanting what you get.

– Dale Carnegie

You can't buy a good reputation; you must earn it.

– Harvey Mackay

Acknowledgments

Our thanks are owed to a large number of people who offered advice, insight and undertook the tedious task of trying to edit and refine our thoughts. Of course the errors and misjudgments within are ours alone.

Michael, Greg, Stephen & Thomas

One of the tests of leadership is the ability to recognize a problem before it becomes an emergency.

– Arnold Glasow

Customers are the reason we open our doors every day, and keep the machines humming all night long. Customers determine what we eat, where we live, whether we stay in business.

– Harvey Mackay

Testimonials

There were several steps when deciding to partner/sell our company. First is of course deciding what are our goals are and why. Then marketing it to people and companies that line up with our goals. Then putting a value on everything we have done for the last 20 + years and having a glimpse of what things are going to look like in the future.

There were some difficult decisions to make but deciding to partner with Equicapitia wasn't one of them. Their motives are clear. They need to make a reasonable return on investment while growing their equity in their acquisition. It makes sense.

How do we make a great living while growing our business, taking advantage of opportunity and not be strapped for cash the whole time.

We were able to take some of our personal equity out of our business while still having cash for growth.

Equicapita was clear on their ability and their intention. They followed through with action and did exactly what they said they would do. I believe they have helped me take the business I love and make it better.

Jon Janssen,
President
North West Crane

When I first learned that a private equity fund was interested in purchasing our company, I was a little concerned. However, after meeting Equicapita and finding out more about their business model, we realized that with Equicapita acting as "custodians" of the company, this was a great opportunity for us. They have invested in the company which keeps us competitive, while maintaining a hands-off approach. Most importantly, the sale process and transition to new ownership has been seamless for both our customers and employees.

Alan van As
General Manager
A & R Metal Industries Ltd.

I have been managing merger and acquisition transactions for over 12 years. Each transaction comes with its own unique circumstances and challenges. Having a knowledgeable buyer is one of the keys to a successful sale transaction.

We recently advised on the sale of a business to Equicapita. Equicapita's knowledge and approach was professional and considerate towards the business owners and our firm. The team ensured that they had a good understanding of the business operations and the goals of our client, not merely focused on the financial performance of the business. We look forward to further transactions with Equicapita.

Wes Priebe
Managing Director
Grant Thornton Corporate Finance Inc.
Edmonton, AB

Over a year after our deal with Equicapita, we are still delighted with our decision to sell to them. It was like a dream come true. We were able to realize the value in our business yet we don't have to worry about the responsibility of owning it anymore. We can move towards our retirement now.

Starting and running a company for 35 years creates value that cannot be duplicated at will. Years of hard work develops know how and customer loyalties that can last a lifetime. Equicapita's business model recognizes that value and capitalizes on it.

The deal provided our employees with job security for now and in the future while ensuring a reliable supplier for our customers going forward. Equicapita fit our company's needs perfectly by supporting current management and allowing Levy's to do what has worked in the past. It was very much a win-win for everyone involved.

It is great for us to know that the company that we have built will continue for years to come while we move forward with our own plans.

Darcy & Kathy Downs
Levy's Machine Works Ltd.

Having had the pleasure to work with Equicapita on a successful transaction, I believe their ability to clearly communicate what was being offered, their sensible methodology of placing appropriate value on intangibles and future worth, and their well-organized due diligence process is what sets them apart in the market.

Andrew Wood
Senior Vice President
BCMS, Corporate Sell-side Advisor

Working with Equicapita has been a seamless transition since our sale. Metercor's management team, which includes two previous owners has continued with "business as usual" with no direct involvement in the day to day operation from Equicapita. Suggestions and decisions have been fully supported allowing Metercor the opportunity for growth.

As a previous owner, now acting as president of Metercor, I still feel pride of ownership and look forward to the success of Metercor and Equicapita.

Len Chappell
President, Metercor Inc.

Our favorite holding period is forever.

— *Warren Buffett*

About the Authors

Michael Cook

Michael is a director of Equicapita. He has over 15 years experience working with private businesses in general business advisory, executive management, sell side advisory, buy side private equity and at the board of director level over a broad range of industries. Michael has worked with private businesses to improve operations, implement financial controls, introduce benchmarking, and to focus on key drivers to increase business value. Mr. Cook holds Chartered Accountant (1999) and Chartered Business Valuator (2002) designations in addition to a BCom. (1993) from the University of Manitoba.

Greg Tooth

Greg is a director of Equicapita. He has over 15 years of experience in commodity trading and private equity. Greg has in-depth experience in energy infrastructure and is a co-founder of an oil and gas investment fund. He has extensive experience sourcing, funding and closing private, mid-market transactions within the SME space. As principal, he led a private investor group in the consolidation of a highly fragmented transportation services business, culminating in the successful acquisition of four Alberta based companies. Greg has a Bachelor of Commerce degree from the University of Alberta (1994) and holds the Chartered Financial Analyst designation (1999).

Stephen Johnston

Stephen is a director of Equicapita. Stephen has over 15 years experience as a private equity fund manager. Stephen was a senior fund manager for a large UK based investment bank managing a CAD$ 500 million emerging market private equity portfolio. Stephen is a regular contributor to various print and television media outlets and his analysis has appeared in Bloomberg, Fortune, Macleans, WSJ, FT, Canadian Business, Business Week, Business News Network, and the Globe and Mail. He is the author of Cantillon's Curse – a book discussing the macro-economic issues facing investors in the post-2008 financial crisis world and a director of the Mises Institute of Canada. Stephen has a BSc. (1987) and a LLB from the University of Alberta (1990) and an MBA (1994) from the London Business School.

Thomas Syvret

Thomas is a Vice President of Equicapita. Thomas spent 12 years at Ernst & Young Chartered Accountants (E&Y). He has over 12 years of experience working with both private and public companies in a financial advisory capacity, including, amongst others, sell-side transaction advisory, buy-side transaction advisory and financing advice. Thomas has worked with companies across a wide array of industries, including, amongst others, energy services, manufacturing, distribution, construction, telecommunications, and retail. A significant proportion of his experience is in the mid-market or SME space. Thomas is a Chartered Accountant (2004) and holds a Bachelor of Business Administration (Honours) from Mount Saint Vincent University.

Business Owner Questionnaire

1. What year was your company founded? What is the story from beginning to today?

2. Where is your principal location? Do you have satellite locations? How many?

3. Please provide last three years financial statements prepared by your accountant.

4. What percentage of revenue or EBITDA do you invest on capital assets in a given year?

5. What is your current and maintainable working capital ratio?

6. What is the age of the principal owner(s) selling the business? What percentage of your workweek are you active in the business?

7. Describe your management team? What are their roles, responsibilities and tenure? What are their long-term plans with respect to staying with the business? Would they consider investing in the business along with the new owners?

8. What is your industry? What is the outlook?

9. Provide a detailed description of your business. Your industry. Your business model – how do you generate revenue? New customers? What is the sales cycle? Are your revenues recurring in nature? What is your approach/strategy to acquiring new business? Do you have sales people?

10. What percentage of revenue do your top 10 customers represent? What is your percentage of recurring customer business?

11. What is your competitive advantage? Do you have a unique selling proposition?

12. How did your business perform in the most recent economic downturn? How resilient is your business to changes in economic activity?

Recommended Reading

Here is a non-comprehensive list of some books you might find interesting or useful adjuncts to what you have read above:

Family Business Succession: The Final Test of Greatness - by Stephen L. McClure, John L. Ward & Craig E. Aronoff

Strategic Planning for the Family Business: Parallel Planning to Unite the Family and Business - by Randel S. Carlock & Craig E Aronoff

Family Business Succession: Your Roadmap to Continuity by Kelly LeCouvie and Jennifer Pendergast

Exiting Your Business, Protecting Your Wealth: A Strategic Guide For Owner's and Their Advisors by John M. Leonetti

Business Succession Planning For Dummies by Arnold Dahlke

The Law by Frederic Bastiat

Economics in One Lesson by Henry Hazlitt

The Black Swan & *Fooled By Randomness* by Nassim Taleb

Lost wealth may be replaced by industry, lost knowledge by study, lost health by temperance or medicine, but lost time is gone forever.

– *Samuel Smiles*

Definitions

Amortization – The process of spreading payments over multiple periods. The term is used for two separate processes: amortization of loans and amortization of intangible assets.

Accounts Payable A/P - An accounting entry that represents an entity's obligation to pay off a short-term debt to its creditors. The accounts payable entry is found on a balance sheet under the heading current liabilities.

Accounts Receivable A/R - Money owed by customers to another entity in exchange for goods or services that have been delivered or used, but not yet paid for. Receivables usually come in the form of operating lines of credit and are usually due within a relatively short time period, ranging from a few days to a year. On a public company's balance sheet, accounts receivable is often recorded as an asset because this represents a legal obligation for the customer to remit cash for its short-term debts.

ASPE - Accounting Standards for Private Enterprises

CIM - A confidential information memorandum is a document drafted by an advisory firm or investment banker used in a sell-side engagement to market a business to prospective buyers. A CIM, also referred to as the "book" will typically include the following: A detailed description of the business and its operations; A summary of the industry and opportunities within the market; Financial information including analysis of historical results and future projections; and a summary of the auction process including the proposed structure of the deal and timing for receipts of expressions of interest or letters of intent. It is crucial that all valuable attributes of the business are highlighted in the CIM to get the best terms and highest possible price.

Claw-back – The term claw-back is typically used to refer to any money or benefits that have been given out but need to be returned due to special circumstances, which are mentioned in a contract.

Collection Period (Days) – Measures the average number of days taken to collect trade debts. The equation is ((Average Receivables / Credit Sales) x 365).

Confidentiality Agreement - A legal agreement between two or more parties that is used to signify that a confidential relationship exists between the parties. A confidentiality agreement is used in strategic meetings where various parties become privy to sensitive corporate information, which should not be made available to the general public or to various competitors. Also known as a "non-disclosure agreement (NDA)".

Current Assets - A balance sheet account that represents the value of all assets that are reasonably expected to be converted into cash within one year in the normal course of business. Current assets include cash, accounts receivable, inventory, marketable securities, prepaid expenses and other liquid assets that can be readily converted to cash.

Current Liabilities - A company's debts or obligations that are due within one year. Current liabilities appear on the company's balance sheet and include short term debt, accounts payable, accrued liabilities and other debts.

Current Ratio - Measures whether the company has sufficient resources to pay its debts over the next 12 months. The equation is (Current Assets / Current Liabilities).

Debt to Equity Ratio (%) - measures the relative proportion of debt used to finance the company's assets. The equation is (Debt / Shareholders Equity).

Depreciation - Depreciation is the process by which a company allocates an asset's cost over the duration of its useful life. Each time a company prepares its financial statements, it records a depreciation expense to allocate a portion of the cost of the buildings, machines or equipment it has purchased to the current fiscal year. The purpose of recording depreciation as an expense is to spread the initial price of the asset over its useful life.

Due diligence – A review and analysis of all aspects of a purchase before signing. Capabilities of the management team, performance record, deal flow, investment strategy and legal/formation documents, are examples of areas that are fully examined during the due diligence process.

Earnings - The amount of profit that a company produces during a specific period, which is usually defined as a quarter (three calendar months) or a year. Earnings typically refer to after-tax net income. Ultimately, a business's earnings are the main determinant of its share price, because earnings and the circumstances relating to them can indicate whether the business will be profitable and successful in the long run.

Earn-out – A mechanism used to bridge a gap in valuation expectations between a buyer and a seller. An earn-out is based on future results of the company post acquisition and is established utilizing a forecast that the vendor believes the company will achieve. An earn-out can be formulated with revenue, gross margin or EBITDA.

EBITDA – Earnings before interest tax, depreciation and amortization

Free Cash Flow - A measure of financial performance calculated as operating cash flow minus capital expenditures. Free cash flow (FCF) represents the cash that a company is able to generate after laying out the money required to maintain or expand its asset base. Free cash flow is important because it allows a company to pursue opportunities that enhance shareholder value. Without cash, it's tough to develop new products, make acquisitions, pay dividends and reduce debt. FCF is calculated as: EBIT(1-Tax Rate) + Depreciation & Amortization - Change in Net Working Capital - Capital Expenditure. It can also be calculated by taking operating cash flow and subtracting capital expenditures.

GAAP - Generally Accepted Accounting Principles

Goodwill - The value of a business attributable to the excess earnings that a business generates over and above that which would be expected to be generated on the net equity in the business.

Gross Profit Margin (%) – Measures how well the company controls its cost of sales. The equation is (Sales minus Cost of Goods Sold / Sales)

General Partner - General partner is a person who joins with at least one other person to form a business. A general partner has responsibility for the actions of the business, can legally bind the business and is personally liable for all the business's debts and obligations.

General Security Agreement - A GSA is a document that provides a lender a security interest in a specified asset or property that is pledged as collateral. In the event that the borrower defaults, the pledged collateral can be seized and sold. A security agreement mitigates the default risk the lender faces.

Hold-back – an amount retained in a trust account after the transaction closes to allow for any post closing adjustments, usually with working capital.

IFRS - International Financial Reporting Standards are designed as a common global standard so that company accounts are understandable and comparable across international boundaries. IFRS is progressively replacing the many different national accounting standards.

In-kind Consideration – Consideration paid at closing not in the form of cash, includes items such as preferred trust units, shares, vendor financing, or earn-out.

Inventory - The raw materials, work-in-process goods and completely finished goods that are considered to be the portion of a business's assets that are ready or will be ready for sale. Inventory represents one of the most important assets that most businesses possess, because the turnover of inventory represents one of the primary sources of revenue generation and subsequent earnings for the company's shareholders/owners.

Inventory Turns – Measures the number of times inventory is sold or used in a year. The equation is the (Cost of Goods Sold / Average Inventory).

Lender - Someone who makes funds available to another with the expectation that the funds will be repaid, plus any interest and/or fees. A lender can be an individual, or a public or private group. Lenders may provide funds for a variety of reasons, such as a mortgage, automobile loan or small business loan.

Letter of Intent ("LOI") - LOIs resemble written contracts, but are usually not binding on the parties. Many LOIs, however, contain provisions that are binding, such as non-disclosure agreements, a covenant to negotiate in good faith, or a "stand-still" or "no-shop" provision promising exclusive rights to negotiate. The most common purposes of an LOI are to clarify the key points of a complex transaction for the convenience of the parties.

Limited Partnership – Two or more partners united to conduct a business jointly, and in which one or more of the partners is liable only to the extent of the amount of money that partner has invested. Limited partners do not receive dividends, but enjoy direct access to the flow of income and expenses.

Mezzanine financing - Mezzanine capital is any subordinated debt or preferred equity instrument that represents a claim on a company's assets which is senior only to that of the common shares. Mezzanine financings can be structured either as debt (typically an unsecured and subordinated note) or preferred stock.

Mutual Fund Trust – A mutual fund trust is a unit trust in which all holdings and transactions in the units comply with the prescribed conditions governing in particular the number of unit holders and the dispersal of ownership of the units. If a trust becomes a mutual fund trust within 90 days after the end of its first taxation year, it may elect to be treated as such from the beginning of that taxation year. Classified by Canada Revenue Agency as a "flow-through entity", this structure allows the taxable income earned inside the trust to be treated such that taxable income flows through to the individual unit holder and be treated at the individual tax rate, which is often lower than the highest marginal tax rate at which it would be taxed if the fund held on to it.

Operating Expenses (%) - Measures the ongoing costs of running the company. The equation is (Operating Costs / Sales).

Nano Gap - The term "nano gap" was coined by accounting firm Deloitte to describe the shortage of capital to fund the retirement of baby-boomer entrepreneurs seeking to sell their small, medium enterprises (SMEs).

Net Income – The total earnings (profit) of a business after costs of sales, operating expenses, depreciation and amortisation, interest expenses and taxes.

Payables Period (Days) – Measures the number of days taken to pay suppliers. The equation is ((Average Payables / Total Supplier Purchases) x 365).

Preferred Dividend - A dividend that is accrued and paid on a company's preferred shares. In the event that a company is unable to pay all dividends, claims to preferred dividends take precedence over claims to dividends that are paid on common shares.

Private equity - Equity capital that is not quoted on a public exchange. Private equity consists of investors and funds that make investments directly into private companies or conduct buyouts of public companies that result in a delisting of public equity. Capital for private equity is raised from retail and institutional investors, and can be used to fund new technologies, expand working capital within an owned company, make acquisitions, or to strengthen a balance sheet.

Quick look reporting – A quick-look report is designed for the owners or upper-management of the company and consists of the important measurements that give you a check on the health of your company. The items to include are the ten key drivers or factors in your business that can be reported on each day that you can have a quick look at to see how the business is doing and by glancing you can see how the results will be next month or 60 days out.

R&D – research and development Return on Assets (%) – Measures how profitable the company's assets are in generating revenue. The equation is (Net Income / Average Assets).

Return on Equity (%) – Measures the rate of return on the ownership interest of the common stock owners. The equation is (Net Income / Shareholder' Equity).

Return on Sales (%) – Measures the company's operational efficiency. The equation is (Earnings Before Interest and Taxes or Operating Income / Sales).

RMA - Risk Management Associates.

Sales to Net Working Capital – Measures how well the company's cash is being used to generate sales. The equation is (Sales / (Accounts Receivable + Inventory – Accounts Payable)).

Shareholder's Agreement – A shareholders' agreement is an agreement amongst the shareholders of a company as to how they will conduct themselves in relation to key issues over and above what is set out in the formation documents.

Shareholders' Equity - A firm's total assets minus its total liabilities. Equivalently, it is share capital plus retained earnings minus treasury shares. Shareholders' equity represents the amount by which a company is financed through common and preferred shares.

Subordinated Debt - A loan that ranks below other loans with regard to claims on assets or earnings. In the case of default, creditors with subordinated debt wouldn't get paid out until after the senior debt holders were paid in full. Therefore, subordinated debt is more risky than unsubordinated debt.

Vendor Take-back – A vendor take back is a type of non-cash consideration often used by buyers to finance the total purchase price of a company. It provides a buyer with a source of financing without having to access the external debt market and pay fees. For the seller, it is a good alternative to receiving cash or stock in the buyer depending on how favourable the interest and terms of the vendor take back are.

Working Capital - A measure of both a company's efficiency and its short-term financial health. The working capital is calculated as: Current Assets – Current Liabilities.

Working Capital Peg – The amount of working capital agreed between vendor and purchaser to be present in the business on closing.

Sources: Wikipedia, Investopedia, Equicapita

Small businesses are the backbone of our communities.

– Tom Allen

You're only as good as the people you hire.

— *Ray Kroc*

Endnotes

1   The Baby Boom generation is defined as those people born between 1946 and 1964 according to the US Census Bureau

2   Northern Trust, It's More Than Just the Numbers, Demographic Shifts & Investment Strategies, June 2010

3   CBC News "Baby boomer retirement glut poses risk"

4   Statscan CANSIM, table 380-0064 (C$1.879 trillion)

5   Canada's Pension Landscape Report, 2012 - C$1.12 trillion 2011

6   Bank of Montreal report published in 2009

7   Ibid.

8   Canadian Federation of Independent Businesses, October 2006

9   Mass Mutual/Raymond Institute, 2002

10 Day, George S. and Robin Wensley, 1988, "Assessing Advantage: A Framework for Diagnosing Competitive Superiority." Journal of Marketing 52 (April): 1-20

11 Bank of Montreal report published in 2009

12 Canadian Federation of Independent Businesses, October 2006

13 Mass Mutual/Raymond Institute, 2002

14 Day, George S. and Robin Wensley, 1988, "Assessing Advantage: A Framework for Diagnosing Competitive Superiority." Journal of Marketing 52 (April): 1-20

If people like you,
they'll listen to you,
but if they trust you,
they'll do business
with you.

— *Zig Ziglar*